More Praise for *Beyond Salt and Pepper*

"Open any page of this new compendium on herbs and spices and you will find something fascinating. Whether it is an historical tidbit or a great culinary tip which you can easily deploy to ramp up the flavor of your favorite recipes, *Beyond Salt and Pepper* is sure to become a favorite kitchen resource."

Nancy Radke
President of Good Food Creative, Inc.
Director of U.S. Information Office of Consorzio del Formaggio Parmigiano Reggiano

"Haney and Keast have created a resource that is a pleasure to read and a welcome gift for both accomplished and novice cooks. With its clear and engaging writing and a simple, attractive format, this is a handy book to 'spice up meals' and answer those odd queries about commonly used herbs and spices. As a seasoned cook and professional recipe developer, I was continuously intrigued with the taste-tempting "Try This" cooking ideas, like adding rosemary to iced tea. That may become my namesake beverage!"

Rosemary Mark
Culinary Consultant and Blogger, GetCookingSimply.com

"Season your knowledge with this collection of fun flora facts. Informatively written, *Beyond Salt and Pepper* does a superb job of communicating the impact plants have made on world history, culture, and medicine."

Danielle Dávila
Landscape Architect and Principal, Environmental Foresight, Inc.

"C.L. and Bonnie lead you on a journey of exploration of herbs and spices. In our fast-paced lives, we need to make food exciting and interesting quickly and they've made it easier for us to do just that. *Beyond Salt and Pepper* is well researched and the information is presented in a way that makes you want to jump up and cook. Included are gentle nudges to "Try This," which are easy ways to explore an herb or spice. The recipes are approachable and easy enough for a mid-week meal and elegant enough for entertaining. Useful and practical, the book is a valuable resource for those who want to explore the world beyond salt and pepper."

Julie Logue-Riordan
Cooking with Julie, Napa Valley

Beyond Salt and Pepper
Forty Fabulous Flavor Enhancers

C. L. Haney
Bonnie Keast

Earthsong Voices
San Ramon, California
www.EarthsongVoices.com

Published by Earthsong Voices
San Ramon, California
www.EarthsongVoices.com

ISBN: 0-9749111-2-7

Printed and bound in the United States of America

Introduction

C.L. and I are a team, although we have very different styles. For instance, when I prepare a meal, I usually just take the ingredients (pre-cut and pre-measured by someone else) out of a package, box, or bag and follow the directions. Voilà, food on the table. Perhaps I might add a little something like a bit of bottled sauce or even a sprig of parsley to "make it mine." C.L., on the other hand, absolutely loves food. She is captivated by the rich variety of colors, textures, and scents of the raw ingredients, and prefers working from scratch to create dishes that are pleasing to both eye and palate.

A while ago C.L. and I got to talking about our next joint venture. Although I was interested in finding out more about spices and herbs, it wasn't because I wanted to make better meals. I had started to research a few herbs and found their folklore and uses through the ages fascinating. C.L., of course, saw great possibilities to expand her pleasure in gourmet cooking (and eating).

This book is a combination of our interests. We begin with a few nuggets of spice history and facts about the basics of salt and pepper. Then you'll find forty additional seasonings, each described with pertinent facts, legends, and some of their past uses. You'll also find a "Try This" section with each seasoning, adding to your knowledge base and inviting you to use the herb or spice in an easy way. In addition, C.L. has developed a variety of yummy recipes especially for the book that make use of various seasonings. Finally, we mention a few references for your further exploration.

In addition to removing some of the mystique around cooking with seasonings beyond salt and pepper, we wanted to share with you some of what we've learned about each of these palate pleasers. We invite you to browse through *Beyond Salt and Pepper* looking for stories about old "friends" that you often use in cooking and hope you become inspired to try new possibilities. Bon appétit!

Table of Contents

Historical Nuggets   11

Salt and Pepper   17

Beyond Salt and Pepper: Forty Fabulous Flavor Enhancers   23

Especially Tasty Recipes   105

    Starters   109

    Entrees   113

    Sides   122

    Rubs, Marinades, Butters, & Sauces 132

    Brunch - Or Any Time   140

    Desserts   143

Helpful Tidbits   147

    Affinity Chart   148

    Growing Your Own   149

    Resources   150

Index   153

About the Authors   161

Historical Nuggets

Historical Nuggets from the Spice World

Herbs are plants, and human beings have always used local plant life as part of their daily meals. Many herbs are fairly adaptable and spread throughout the world as people migrated and brought with them seeds and cuttings of their favorites. For the most part, our ancestors found that using herbs was pretty much a pick-and-eat proposition.

Not so with spices. Spice plants are much pickier than herbs about where they grow and often need much processing such as cracking, drying, or fermenting before they can be used in foods. Because of the need for just the right combination of heat, moisture, and soil conditions, people found it was not easy to transplant the particular spice they desired. When something is relatively rare, it becomes more valuable. In the case of spices, this value opened trade routes, spurred exploration, and started wars. Here are just a few interesting facts about the influence of spices on world history.

- The word "spice" comes from a word that means "kinds of goods." True to their name, spices have been traded for over two millennia as goods for use in medicines, foods, and rituals. Because of their value and the difficulty in obtaining them, they were used as part of sacraments long before they were thought of as seasonings.

- Egyptian records from before 2500 BC show evidence of the use of specific spices that could only have been obtained from distant places in Asia and the Indonesian Islands.

- It was hunger for spices that launched some of the world-changing events in history, including the opening of important sea routes across the Indian Ocean and around Africa, as well as the connecting of Europe with the New World.

- The Arabian Peninsula is located at the crossroads of Europe, Africa, and Asia. For many of the years during and after the time of Christ, the Arabs had clear monopoly of the spice trade. A spice route gradually evolved into a sea route linking Arabia with China, India, and the Spice Islands.

- Once the Romans figured out that it was possible to sail from Egypt to India and back, the Arabic monopoly was broken for a few centuries. However, Muhammad, founder of the Islam religion, married the widow of a spice trader. He understood that by solidifying a hold on existing spice trade routes, both the Islamic religion and economy could prosper. The Arabs thus controlled the spice trade once again, and Islam spread along spice routes throughout much of the known world.

- The Crusades began in the 1090s. Many knights returned to Europe with treasure chests filled with peppercorns and spices, and recipes from the Crusader centuries show many highly spiced dishes.

- For a few centuries during Europe's Dark Ages, there was almost no access to the spice market for Europeans. Gradually, however, the seaports of Genoa and Venice rose to power and were able to trade for, and then transport spices across the Mediterranean Sea from Alexandria. Of course, these spices were so expensive that only the very rich could afford them.

- Over the next few centuries, Spain, Portugal, the Netherlands, England, and France built colonial holdings around the globe and vied for supremacy. Columbus sailed from Spain to the Caribbean Islands and thought he had found India. Five years later, da Gama sailed from Portugal and did reach India, thus effectively breaking the Venetian monopoly. While Spain and Portugal struggled for supremacy in the spice trade, Britain and France chose privateering as a way to gain the valuable spices.

- For many centuries, particular spices could only be grown in one small geographic area. Once discovered by an explorer and brought back to his home country, that spice became extremely valuable and greed and savagery took over. For instance, the Dutch "convinced" the leaders of the islands of Banda that complete control of the nutmeg trade belonged to the Dutch East India Company. To enforce this, the Dutch killed more than forty leaders of the Banda people, beheaded them, and posted their heads on bamboo spears.

- The desire for a foothold on the Spice Islands caused the Dutch Republic to trade what has become the island of Manhattan to the English in 1667 in return for the Island of Run for its nutmegs.

- Wars continued for several centuries, motivated partly by the profits of spice trading. During this time countries gradually transplanted trees, often stolen, from their place of origin to their own colonial holdings. By the start of the nineteenth century, monopolies no longer existed and the spice trade was truly international.

Think of it. The cuisines of various countries of the world developed in part because of people's desire to conquer other peoples. For example, as the Arabians spread into India, they brought with them cumin and coriander. Those spices, combined with the pepper, ginger, and turmeric of the native Indian people, make the base of many of today's South Asian dishes. Centuries later, along came the British who combined both groups of spices. British sailors then spread what we now know as curry throughout the world.

Thus the power struggles of the world are responsible for bringing us many of the seasonings we enjoy today, and for that, we are grateful.

Salt & Pepper

Salt

Salt is a mineral that is essential in small amounts for the survival of all living creatures. It is obtained from sea water or mined from rock deposits.

Fun Facts and Folklore

- During Roman times, salt was used as currency and the Latin word *salarium* (payment made in salt) is the root of our word "salary." Roman soldiers were paid partly in salt, as it had high value and could be traded. The phrases "salt of the earth" and "worth one's salt" also speak to the value of salt.

- The Arabs established great salt trading corridors. One caravan route began with salt on the Mediterranean coast and traveled along the Sahara desert, returning with gold dust, ivory, goat skins, and slaves.

- As a natural preservative, salt has been used throughout the ages to ensure the safe storage and transport of food. Modern processed foods often have a very high salt content.

- Salt has often been taxed throughout human history. Chinese records from the twentieth century BC record salt taxes. In Colonial America, Thomas Paine complained of the English salt taxes. Mohandas Gandhi led India's non-violent salt march in order to challenge the British-imposed monopoly on salt.

- There are many kinds of salt beyond the well-known table salt, each having a slightly different texture and flavor. Kosher salt has a large surface area and is preferred by many chefs for cooking. Rock salt is used in making ice cream as it quickens the freezing process. Unrefined sea salts have different flavors and textures, depending on their origin. Hawaiian, *sel gris*, *fleur de sel*, Maldon, and Himalayan are just a few of the finishing and specialty salts used to enhance the flavor of foods.

Try This!

- Consider using unsalted butter when recipes call for butter. That way you can add whatever flavors of salt will heighten the food's flavor.

- Make your own herbed salt. To one cup of unrefined sea salt add a teaspoon of any or several of the following: rosemary, oregano, thyme, basil, dill, chives, sage, celery seed, marjoram, lavender buds, or dried parsley.

- When a dish tastes overly salty, try adding a pinch of sugar. A squirt of lemon juice or vinegar can also do the trick.

Pepper

Pepper is the world's most popular spice. Grape-like clusters grow on a flowering vine native to South India. Now cultivated in many tropical regions, pepper's largest producer is currently Vietnam.

Fun Facts and Folklore

- Pepper was considered precious in ancient times and was weighed like gold. Alaric the Visigoth demanded three thousand pounds of pepper in AD 410 as ransom for the city of Rome.

- Often called the "King of Spices," pepper was the core of the European spice traffic. The Age of Exploration began when other countries wanted to get in on an Arab and Venetian monopoly of the spice trade.

- Pepper is unique in that the pepper fruits are marketed in four different versions. Depending on when the fruits are picked and how they are processed, pepper can be black, white, green, or red. In principle, all could be produced from the same pepper plant.

- Black pepper is harvested green, then cooked briefly in boiling water, which causes fermentation and blackening. It is then dried at moderate temperature either in the sun or by machine. White pepper is the seed with the fruit removed. The fully-ripened fruit soaks in water for about a week, then is dried. Green pepper is harvested before it ripens. It is processed by pickling or by quick drying to prevent fermentation. Red pepper is more pungent and aromatic than green pepper and is usually preserved in brine or vinegar.

Try This!

- Most savory recipes call for fresh ground pepper "to taste," so experiment with different amounts.

- For a delicious beef or tuna steak, press a combination of coarsely ground black, white, and red peppercorns into a thick filet and sauté in olive oil or butter.

- Pepper can be even used with sweets. Try putting a pinch of black pepper with a fruit salad or add a dash of pepper to a dark chocolate concoction or over chocolate ice cream. You can also steep a few peppercorns in maple syrup to top your pancakes.

Beyond Salt & Pepper

Seasonings

The word "seasoning" comes from the early French language. It carries with it a sense of ripening and bringing to maturity. As the word was first used during the late 1300s, its meaning also included improving the taste of foods by adding condiments and spices. Now both casual cooks and chefs of haute cuisine use herbs and spices to add flavor, texture, and aroma to their dishes.

The word "herb" comes from Latin *herba*, which means grass. Herbs are the leafy, green parts of aromatic, temperate-climate plants and are used fresh or dried to increase flavor in foods. Although most herbs are chopped or sliced just before adding them to a dish, cooks sometimes use the whole stalk of herbs to enhance taste in stews or soups, or they may add whole leaves as part of a salad. Many herbs are also used as garnishes.

Spices are parts of tropical plants. They may come from the berries, bark, flower, roots, or seeds of the plant. Spices are often processed before use by drying, grinding into powder, or curing.

Some plants have both herb and spice components. For instance, coriander leaf (usually called cilantro) is an herb while the coriander seed is a spice.

Most herbs and spices can be described by their predominant characteristic, such as bitter, herbaceous, peppery, nutty, or sweet. It is also helpful to keep in mind their relative strength, which can help you determine how much or little to use in a dish.

Strong herbs and spices can overpower more delicate flavors if used indiscriminately; therefore, you can employ them sparingly. Strong seasonings include bay leaf, cayenne pepper, cumin, garlic, ginger, horseradish, mustard, and rosemary.

Herbs and spices with medium flavors can be added in moderate amounts. Depending on the main food ingredient in your dish, this can be about a teaspoon of dried or two to three teaspoons of fresh seasoning for six servings. Medium seasonings include allspice, basil, caraway, cinnamon, dill, fennel seed, marjoram, mint, oregano, sage, savory, tarragon, thyme, and turmeric.

Delicate herbs and spices are mild in flavor and combine well with many other herbs and spices. As such, you can use them liberally in your cooking. Chervil, chives, and parsley are examples of delicate seasonings.

A number of herbs and spices are considered "sweet" in nature. By utilizing them in sweet dishes, you may be able to reduce the amount of sugar you use. Consider incorporating allspice, anise, cinnamon, cloves, ginger, mint, mace, star anise, and vanilla into your sweet dish preparation.

As with most cooking, however, there is no "right" and "wrong," because seasoning is a matter of taste – your taste. Come and explore the wonderful world of herbs and spices and experiment for yourself!

Allspice

Allspice is an aromatic, pea-sized berry. Each berry contains two small seeds that give off the aromas of cinnamon, cloves, and nutmeg. Growing on the evergreen pimiento tree, which is indigenous to South and Central American rain forests, it is the only spice grown exclusively in the Western Hemisphere.

Fun Facts and Folklore

- Christopher Columbus discovered allspice in the Caribbean. Never having seen real pepper, he thought that allspice was the spice he was looking for, and named it "pimienta," the Spanish name for pepper.

- Caribbean natives used allspice to help cure and preserve meats. Allspice-cured meat was know as "boucan" in the language of the Arawaks. Later, Europeans who cured meat this way came to be known as "boucaniers" which ultimately became "buccaneers."

- Allspice contains skin-warming tannins. In the Napoleonic Wars of 1812, Russian soldiers put allspice in their boots to keep their feet warm.

- Allspice is often called Jamaican pepper. Jamaica produces the finest allspice and has long dominated the world market.

Try This!

- For a unique seasoning, try adding a few whole allspice berries to your pepper grinder along with the more common black, white, and green peppercorns.

- A few pinches of ground allspice add a depth of flavor to ground meats and barbecue sauces. Or try adding a teaspoon of the spice to your meatballs.

- Allspice also enhances the flavor of several vegetables, such as squash, sweet potatoes, cabbage, beets, carrots, and spinach. Sprinkle ground allspice over the cooked vegetable, or add it to the vegetable's cooking liquid.

- Add a few allspice berries per cup of liquid when poaching seafood or fruit.

Anise

Anise – not to be confused with Star Anise, which is an entirely different plant – is a tall, feathery annual in the parsley family. It originated in the eastern Mediterranean and its tiny, oval greenish-brown seeds have a sweet licorice flavor.

Fun Facts and Folklore

- Anise is one of the oldest cultivated spices. Early Egyptians, Greeks, and Romans used and enjoyed it. For example, to ward off indigestion, first century Romans ate a special cake flavored with anise and baked in bay leaves. Many also used it as a morning breath freshener.

- Anise became so valuable in early England that King Edward I taxed it, and those taxes helped pay for maintenance and repairs to the London Bridge.

- The book of Matthew in the Bible mentions paying tithe with anise.

- People once believed that anise could ward off the Evil Eye and keep away nightmares if put under one's pillow. It was also believed that the distilled oil of anise, when dabbed on a fishing lure, would improve the fisherman's chances.

- Anise is used to flavor alcoholic drinks such as Arak and Ouzo as well as to scent soaps and perfumes.

- Dogs are attracted by the smell of anise and it is often used as an ingredient in dog food. Anti-blood sport groups use the seeds to put hounds off a scent.

Try This!

- Brushing rolls or sugar cookies with a beaten egg white and dusting them with anise seeds before baking will give baked goods a delightful licorice flavor.

- Sprinkle anise seeds on cooked beets, cabbage, carrots, or cauliflower. Also, melon and anise go well together.

- Add anise to the liquid used to braise beef.

- With cinnamon, caraway seeds, and a pinch of nutmeg, anise creates a pleasant tea.

Basil

Basil is an annual herb belonging to the mint family. Native to India and Asia, it has been cultivated for more than five thousand years and is a key ingredient in Mediterranean cooking.

Fun Facts and Folklore

- In ancient Rome, the name for the herb referred to a fire-breathing dragon, and taking the herb was thought to be a charm against the beast. Today, basil is used as an antidote to venom.

- In Crete, basil meant "love washed with tears," and in some parts of Italy and Romania it was a love token, while in India the herb was sacred and said to have protective powers against evil.

- In Renaissance England, hostesses gave small pots of basil as presents to visitors. They believed basil would keep flies away.

- Burning sprigs of basil on the barbeque is said to deter mosquitos.

- There are more than twelve varieties of basil cultivated for culinary use, and it is one of the easiest cooking herbs to grow. Pinching back the top and cutting off any flower spikes will keep growth abundant throughout summer and into fall.

Try This!

- Use basil leaves as some of your leafy greens in a salad, particularly one that contains either tomatoes or cheese.

- Try adding dried basil to your beef or vegetable stew.

- Combine chopped fresh basil, pine nuts, garlic, and olive oil for a quick pesto sauce. Use with cooked pasta, sliced tomatoes, or as a sandwich spread.

- When you bake fruit pies, tear a basil leaf or two into tiny bits and scatter them over the bottom crust before adding the filling.

"Pounding fragrant things – particularly garlic, basil, parsley – is a tremendous antidote to depression."
Patience Gray, cookery author

Bay

Bay laurel is a small tree growing to between twenty-five and sixty feet, depending on climate. It is indigenous to Asia but adapted early to the climate of the Mediterranean. The terms "bay" and "laurel" are used interchangeably. With its cream-colored blossoms, which bees love, the bay tree is an attractive and useful addition to the garden.

Fun Facts and Folklore

- In ancient Greece and Rome, heroes, poets, and winning athletes were crowned with a garland of laurel leaves as a symbol of achievement. We still use the term "poet-laureate" to honor poets today. The modern term "bachelor" for academic degrees is probably derived from *baccalaureus* (laurel-berry).

- Bay leaves are mildly narcotic. Priestesses at the ancient Temple at Delphi would eat whole bay leaves before giving their prophesies.

- Homer mentions bay laurel both as an herb and medicine used by Ulysses in the epic *Odyssey*.

- The Bedouins in parts of the Saharan Desert use bay leaves to flavor their coffee.

Try This!

- Dried bay leaves are sharp and can cause discomfort to the mouth and throat. Use them for flavoring only, and remove them before serving your dish.

- Bay leaves add depth of flavor to soups, stews, shellfish, pickling brines, sauces, marinades, poultry, and fish.

- Try adding a bay leaf or two when cooking beans or lentils.

- Add a bay leaf to the water you use for cooking carrots or potatoes.

- Bay tree twigs make flavorful skewers for fish shish kebabs.

- When making sweet custards, add a bay leaf to the milk or cream as you simmer it. Remove the leaf before adding other ingredients.

Capers

Native to the Middle East and Mediterranean regions of the world, capers are actually the pickled buds of a bramble-like shrub closely related to members of the cabbage family.

Fun Facts and Folklore

- Capers have been an integral part of Mediterranean cuisine for thousands of years and were often used as an informal currency among merchants traveling the ancient trade routes.

- Caper bushes grow spontaneously in cracks and crevices of rocks and stone walls. They are salt-tolerant and thrive along shores near sea-spray zones. In fact, the ash from burned caper roots has been used as a source of salt.

- Capers require manual labor as they must be picked just as they reach proper size. After the buds are picked, they are usually wilted in the sun for a day or two, graded by size, then preserved in vinegar, brine, wine, or salt.

Try This!

- Mince a few capers and sprinkle over sliced tomatoes.

- A few chopped capers add piquancy to egg or tuna salad.

- You can also chop a few small capers and mix them with melted butter and a squeeze of lemon, for use as a garnish for green beans or fish.

- Capers add a bit of bite to macaroni and cheese casseroles.

Think about the flavor of the main ingredient of a dish. As a rule, the weaker the flavor of the food, the less seasoning you will need to have pleasingly balanced flavors. (Some contestants on the TV show Chopped *have learned this to their detriment!)*

Caraway

Caraway "seed" is actually the dried fruit of a biennial member of the parsley family. It has a nutty, anise flavor and is native to Europe and western Asia. Currently Holland is the world's largest producer. It is a common flavoring in many kinds of rye bread and also used in sauerkraut, sausage, cheese, cabbage, and soups.

Fun Facts and Folklore

- An old superstition holds that caraway seeds prevent the theft of any object which contains them. It was used to keep fowl, pigeons, and lovers from straying.

- Caraway seed cakes were given by farmers to their laborers at feasts celebrating the end of wheat-sowing.

- Shakespeare mentions caraway seeds in his play *Henry IV,* and at Trinity College in Cambridge, the custom of serving roasted apples with a little dish of caraway is still kept.

- Several centuries ago, caraway "comfits" were popular in England. These were little sugar candies with a caraway seed in the center. They were used as both a digestive and a sweet.

Try This!

- ☺ Lightly toast caraway seeds and add them to cheese dishes, cabbage, or potato salad.

- ☺ Mix melted butter with caraway seeds as a spread for French bread or a sauce for green beans.

- ☺ After lightly toasting, sprinkle caraway seeds on egg noodles.

- ☺ Make a bit of "caraway tea" to flavor gravies and sauces. For each cup of tea, steep a couple of pinches of caraway seeds in boiling water.

Use whole spices in dishes that need lengthy cooking. This gives plenty of time for the flavor to blend through the entire recipe.

Cardamom

A member of the ginger family, cardamom is a perennial herb with a thick, fleshy root which sends flowering stems six to twelve feet high. The fruit itself is a small capsule with eight to sixteen brown seeds that are used as the spice. The plant is native to India and southeastern Asia, and the spice is a staple in Mideastern, North African, and Scandinavian cooking.

Fun Facts and Folklore

- Cardamom was first used around the eighth century. Ancient Egyptians chewed it as a tooth cleaner, while ancient Indians regarded it as a cure for obesity. The Greeks and Romans used cardamom as a perfume, and the Vikings introduced the seeds to Scandinavia, where they are often used today in baking.

- Known as the "Queen of Spices," cardamom is a traditional flavoring in Turkish coffee and Indian curry blends.

- Cardamom forms a flavoring and basis for medicinal preparations treating indigestion and flatulence.

- In Mideastern Arab countries, cardamom-flavored coffee is a symbol of generous hospitality.

- Cardamom is one of the most expensive spices by weight, second only to saffron. Although little is needed to impart flavor, it is best to buy whole pods as ground cardamom quickly loses its flavor. Remove the seeds and crush them, discarding the pod.

Try This!

- Add a pinch of ground cardamom, cinnamon, ginger, and cloves to couscous.

- Give applesauce a little more depth of flavor with a dash of ground cardamom.

- Toss a few crushed pods of cardamom into stews or vegetable dishes to add a spicy, sharp seasoning.

- Coffee takes on new dimensions with a pinch of ground cardamom added to your cup.

- When making a chocolate cake, add a couple of pinches of ground cardamom with the flour for subtle added flavor.

Cayenne Pepper

Cayenne pepper is a finely ground powder made from the dried pods of pungent chili peppers. Its supposed center of origin is the Cayenne region of French Guyana. The cayenne chili pepper is now mostly grown in India, East Africa, the Americas, and the West Indies.

Fun Facts and Folklore

- Spanish explorers looking for black pepper misnamed the chilies they found in the new world "pepper." Eager to prove they had indeed opened a new direct sea route to Asia, they brought back samples of the various spices they found in the New World, including "pepper."

- The fruit of the cayenne has been a part of medical treatments for centuries. It is used worldwide to treat a variety of health conditions, including poor circulation, weak digestion, and heart disease.

- Cayenne pepper can be used as a spice in cooking or as a condiment at the table. It particularly enhances the taste of seafood.

- The heat of the cayenne pepper comes from the capsaicin, and according to some medical herbalists, cayenne is more powerful than any other herb or spice, especially at stimulating blood circulation.

Try This!

- Try adding a pinch of cayenne pepper to vegetable dips, casseroles, or salad dressings for extra zip.

- Add a pinch of cayenne pepper to eggs mixed with chopped tomatoes and onions for a tasty breakfast.

- When making breading mixtures for fish or chicken, try adding a dash of cayenne pepper to the mix.

- A pinch of cayenne pepper in chocolate confections will add zest and enhance the chocolate flavors.

When you check foods for seasoning, be sure to use your whole mouth, as different parts of your tongue are sensitive to different tastes. Sweetness, for example, is perceived on the front top part of the tongue, while bitterness registers more on the back. The front of the tongue is also most sensitive to salty, and the back picks up sour flavors.

Chervil

Chervil, a member of the parsley family, is a small, low-growing annual. It is native to eastern Europe and western Asia.

Fun Facts and Folklore

- Ancient Greeks used chervil in spring tonics. As it is a spring herb, it has a natural affinity for other spring foods.

- In Latin, its name means "festive herb" or "herb of joy." In the first century, Pliny used chervil as a seasoning, and the Romans brought it to France, where it is also known as "gourmet's parsley."

- Chervil is said to symbolize sincerity.

- In Norway and France, people liberally sprinkle minced fresh chervil leaves on salad, soups, and stews.

- Chervil prefers cool, moist, and shaded locations. It has a short growing season but pinching off the tops and making successive plantings will give a longer harvest.

- Chervil's delicate flavor is easily preserved in white wine vinegar. When added to foods as a vinaigrette, little else is needed for flavor.

Try This!

- Use chopped chervil on top of potato, tomato, and pea soups, on cooked carrots or cauliflower, or in your favorite spring salad mix.

- Include fresh chervil leaves when making sauces for meat or vegetables. Be sure to add them at the very end of cooking time.

- Dried or frozen chervil leaves add flavor to salad dressings and to egg or mushroom dishes.

- With its finely serrated leaves, chervil makes an attractive garnish for finished dishes.

Chives

Chives are a hardy perennial and the smallest member of the onion family. They are native to Asia and Europe and, unlike regular onions, they have no bulb. The leaves hold the delicate onion flavor.

Fun Facts and Folklore

- For Romanian gypsies, chives were used as part of fortune-telling rituals. They were also believed to drive away evil influences and disease when hung in dried bunches around the house.

- There are Chinese recipes using chives that date back nearly five thousand years. Although chives grow in the wild and were probably used in ancient times, they have only been cultivated in Europe since the Middle Ages. They are believed to have been brought to Europe from China by Marco Polo.

- Early Dutch settlers in America planted chives in the meadows where they pastured cows in order to get chive-flavored milk.

- Chives are supposed to protect roses from black spot and Japanese beetles when planted nearby.

- Chives are only referred to in the plural because they grow in clumps rather than alone. Chives lose their flavor when cooked so use them raw whenever possible.

Try This!

- Chives' mild onion flavor will enhance the taste of yogurt, butter, cream cheese, and baked potatoes.

- Try snipping chives over cooked eggs for a subtle, onion-flavored garnish.

- Add a generous amount of chopped chives to your stuffing for zucchini or peppers.

- The lavender or pink chive flowers are edible so use them raw in a salad or fold them into an omelet.

"Cooking with herbs is like icing a cake: it makes a dish complete." Mountain Family Growers

Chocolate

Chocolate comes from cacao beans, the fruit of the cacao tree. The beans must be fermented, dried, roasted, and ground before they become chocolate as we know it. Although native to the Americas, cocoa trees now produce beans in Africa, Asia, and islands of the Pacific.

Fun Facts and Folklore

- The earliest use of cacao beans was around 1100 BC in Central and South America, where they were used as the main ingredient in chocolate beverages for royalty, as ceremonial insturments, and as currency. In the Aztec system, a turkey was worth one hundred cacao beans while an avocado was worth three beans. There were even counterfeit beans, carved out of clay.

- During the 1600s, the Catholic Church declared that eating chocolate did not break a fast. My thoughts exactly.

- The Marquis de Sade used chocolate to disguise the taste of poisons, while Casanova used chocolate with champagne to seduce women.

- Chocolate is part of the genus *Theobroma*, which means "food of the gods."

- During World War II, the United States government commissioned the Hershey Company to create a candy bar to be included with each soldier's rations.

- Chocolate contains the stimulants caffeine and theobromine, as well as serotonin and other nutrients which act as a tonic for the human spirit.

Try This!

 Try using small pieces of baking chocolate in sauces with a tomato base.

 You might make cocoa powder one of your ingredients in rubs for chicken, beef, or pork.

 Experiment with adding black pepper, chilies, anise, cardamom or a bit of orange peel to your chocolate concoctions.

 Try dipping any of the following in dark or milk chocolate melted in a double boiler: pound cake, strawberries, pineapple chunks, nuts, candied ginger, pretzels, cheese, or even potato chips. What an easy dessert!

Cilantro

Cilantro is the leafy part of an aromatic herb in the carrot family. Originally grown around present-day Greece, the seeds of the plant are known as coriander. Although cilantro resembles flat-leaf parsley, a sniff will tell the difference.

Fun Facts and Folklore

- The cilantro plant is said to have grown in the Hanging Gardens of Babylon.

- There is evidence that ancient Egyptians used cilantro in their soups.

- To some, cilantro tastes like soap, and a group numbering in the hundreds have formed an anti-cilantro society. One might say they have "cilantrophobia."

- Folk medicine includes the use of cilantro to relieve anxiety and insomnia.

- Fresh cilantro leaves are frequently used in Asian and Latin American dishes.

- The Chinese call cilantro "fragrant greens" and add it to stir-frys for its fresh and pungent taste.

Try This!

- Although available in dried form, cilantro is best used fresh. Stir minced cilantro into cooked rice.

- Chop cilantro leaves to sprinkle over sautéed carrots, or use as a garnish with carrot soup.

- Use whole cilantro leaves as part of your salad greens mixture.

To become familiar with the essence of a specific herb, treat it like a fine wine. Lightly rub a leaf and check the scent. Thoughtfully taste its flavor by chewing a clean leaf. No need to swallow.

Cinnamon

Cinnamon is the inner bark of a tropical evergreen tree. It is harvested during the rainy season when it is pliable, then dried into curly sticks or ground into powder. True cinnamon is native to Sri Lanka, while the cinnamon used in North America usually comes from the cassia tree grown in Vietnam, China, Indonesia, and Central America.

Fun Facts and Folklore

- Used as both a flavoring for beverages and an embalming agent in ancient Egypt, cinnamon was considered more precious than gold. To be fair, gold was in abundance at that time and used commonly as an ornamental metal.

- The Romans believed the fragrance of cinnamon was sacred and burned it at funerals. The emperor Nero burned a year's supply of cinnamon on his wife Poppaca's funeral pyre. This extravagant gesture was meant to signify the depth of his grief.

- For centuries the Arabs maintained a monopoly of the spice by claiming that cinnamon was harvested from the nests of ferocious birds and had to be gathered under their attack.

- Because cinnamon, along with pepper, was so sought after by fifteenth century Europeans, some say the search for cinnamon led indirectly to the discovery of America.

- Cinnamon was a staple ingredient in medieval Europe. Since most meals were prepared in a single cauldron, casseroles containing both meat and fruit were common and cinnamon helped bridge the flavors. Mince pie is a typical combination which has survived to this day.

Try This!

- For a healthy dessert, try sprinkling cinnamon on freshly cut oranges, apples, peaches, or apricots.

- Cooked vegetables, such as carrots and spinach, also benefit from a light dusting of cinnamon, or use a cinnamon stick in the cooking water.

- Put a dash of cinnamon in meatloaf mixtures for a faintly exotic note. Or add sticks of cinnamon to stews, broths, or pastas as they simmer. Remove before serving.

- Cinnamon also partners beautifully with chocolate in desserts or drinks.

Cloves

Clove is the dried flower bud of the clove tree, an evergreen indigenous to the Moluccas, once known as the Spice Islands. The name itself is derived from the Latin word for nail because of clove's shape.

Fun Facts and Folklore

- The first mention of clove in literature referred to it as the "chicken-tongue" spice. This was in the third century BC in China, and referred to its hot, pungent flavor. It was also written that courtiers were expected to keep cloves in their mouths while addressing the emperor to avoid offending him with bad breath.

- Natives in the Molucca Islands planted a clove tree for each child born. They believed the fate of the tree was aligned with the fate of that child. When the Dutch set fire to clove trees and raised prices in 1816 to protect their world monopoly, the natives revolted and changed the politics of the area forever.

- In 1760, large quantities of cloves were burned in Amsterdam to keep up prices of this spice.

- Clove is the only spice that is smoked more than it is eaten. More than half of the world's clove production is ground with tobacco to make *kretek*. These popular cigarettes are smoked by nearly every male in Indonesia.

Try This!

- Like the familiar clove-decorated ham, tea and wine can also gain flavor from the addition of cloves.

- Make an interesting tomato soup using tomatoes, beef broth, and a few cloves per cup of soup. Strain out the cloves before serving.

- Drop a few cloves in rice while it is cooking (remove before serving), or drop a pinch of ground cloves into a scrambled egg mixture.

- Flavor stock with a clove-studded onion, or add ground cloves to a pot of baked beans or to chicken dishes.

Enhance the flavors of spices by buying small amounts of whole spices and lightly toasting them before grinding the amount you need.

Coriander

Coriander is an annual herb, native to Southern Europe and the Middle East. Coriander is the name given to the dried seeds of the plant, while the leaves are known as cilantro.

Fun Facts and Folklore

- The word coriander comes from a Greek word meaning "stinky bug" that may either refer to the strong smell the plant gives off when it is bruised or to the fact that the young seed resembles a bedbug in shape.

- Ancient Hebrews originally used cilantro root as the bitter herb in the symbolic Passover meal. The Old Testament mentions that the manna eaten by the Israelites when they returned from slavery in Egypt tasted like coriander seeds.

- Roman legions in Britain mixed coriander with vinegar and cumin to preserve meat and carried it as flavoring for their bread made on the march. In Medieval Europe, coriander seeds were widely used because of their ability to make spoiled meats palatable by masking their rotting flavor.

- Chinese folklore holds that the seeds of a coriander plant have the power to bestow immortality.

- Coriander seeds lose their disagreeable scent as they dry and become more fragrant the longer they are kept.

Try This!

- ☺ Coriander, along with turmeric and cumin, is a key ingredient in many forms of curry, which is used to flavor meats and casseroles.

- ☺ Try adding a little ground coriander to cooking lentils, beans, or pea soup, or use it as part of a rub for poultry or fish.

- ☺ A dash of coriander on cooked beets adds zest.

- ☺ Sprinkle a teaspoon of ground coriander over the apples when making an apple pie.

You can enhance the taste of low-salt or no-cholesterol foods by adding herbs and spices. For instance, add a teaspoon each of coriander, cumin, and dried oregano to vegetable soup.

Cumin

Cumin, a member of the parsley family, is a native of Egypt and grows now in most hot climates. Cumin seeds are actually the small dried fruit of this annual plant. The spicy cumin flavor is well known in Mexican, Thai, Vietnamese, Moroccan, and Indian cuisine, and is a key component of both chili and curry powders.

Fun Facts and Folklore

- Cumin is mentioned in the Bible as a seasoning for soup and bread and also as a currency used to pay tithes to the priests. In Egypt it was used both as a culinary spice and for the mummification of pharaohs.

- Greek and Roman students used cumin medicinally and cosmetically to induce a pallid complexion in an effort to convince their teachers they had pulled "all-nighters" to study for class.

- During the Middle Ages, cumin was a symbol of love and fidelity. People carried cumin in their pockets when attending wedding ceremonies. Superstition held that cumin kept chickens and lovers from straying, and married soldiers were sent off to war with a loaf of cumin bread baked by their wives.

Try This!

- ☺ Heat cumin and minced garlic in olive oil and drizzle the mixture over cooked vegetables or potatoes.

- ☺ Add ground cumin to the water used to cook beans, rice, couscous, or lentils. Cumin is also a great addition to chili.

- ☺ Cumin pairs perfectly with lamb, so consider using it as part of your rub, or add a little ground cumin to the lamb's cooking juices when making a sauce or gravy.

- ☺ Sprinkle a pinch of ground cumin over egg dishes for a subtle Southwestern effect.

Store spices away from warm places because heat promotes evaporation of the essential oils that give spices their zing.

Dill

Dill is a bright green, feathery annual and a member of the parsley family. It is native to the Mediterranean region and western Asia. Its seeds are used as a spice and its leaves as an herb.

Fun Facts and Folklore

- Derived from the Norse word *dilla* which means "to lull," dill was once given to crying babies to soothe them. The dill seed contains an oil that relaxes muscles, especially digestive muscles. For centuries people have used dill in various forms to cure indigestion, nausea, and colic.

- Romans thought dill was an effective stimulant for gladiators, while the Talmud required that tithes be paid on the seeds, leaves, and stems of the dill plant.

- People in ancient Greece considered dill a sign of wealth. They even flaunted their wealth by burning dill-scented oil.

- During the Middle Ages dill was used as an ingredient in love potions and as protection against evil and witchcraft, while magicians used it in their charms and spells.

- Dill is a fast-growing, hardy, and drought-resistant annual. The seeds need to be sown directly in the soil, as dill does not like to be transplanted. This herb has two seasons: in spring its leaves are wonderfully tasty, while in fall its seeds ripen.

Try This!

- Dill's most well-known use, as a pickling ingredient for cucumbers, is at least four hundred years old.

- Sprinkle chopped dill over cooked peas and carrots, fresh coleslaw, cucumber salad, or a bowl of tomato soup.

- Dill has a natural affinity for root vegetables such as carrots, potatoes, turnips, and beets. Add a sprinkling of dill seeds to their cooking liquid.

- Try adding dried dill weed to a pot roast as it cooks.

You can chop herbs that have soft leaves, then freeze them with a little oil in ice cube trays for later use.

Fennel Seeds

Fennel is a hardy perennial, considered native to the Mediterranean but widely grown throughout the world. It grows to a height of about five feet and the leaves and seeds are used for seasoning, while the bulb-like base is cooked as a vegetable. The fennel plant is a relative of anise, dill, and cumin, and its licorice-flavored seeds are often confused with anise.

Fun Facts and Folklore

- The ancient Greeks referred to fennel by the name "marathon." The important Battle of Marathon was named after the plants that grew on the battlefield.

- According to Greek mythology, Prometheus stole fire from the gods and smuggled it to the human race inside the hollow stem of a fennel stalk.

- During Medieval times, fennel, together with St. John's Wort and other herbs, was thought to counteract witchcraft spells. People hung it over their doors on Midsummer's Eve to ward off evil spirits.

- The Puritans chewed fennel seeds to hold off hunger during fasts and long worship services.

- Today, fennel seeds are often used in place of tarragon in *herbes de Provence*. They may also be used in curry, and are one of the Chinese five-spice ingredients. In India the seeds are coated with a brightly colored candy and served after meals as a digestive and a treatment for flatulence.

Try This!

- ◉ Try using fennel seeds when poaching fish or other seafood, or grind a few seeds to include with other herbs in a rub for fish, pork, or lamb.

- ◉ You might also add ground fennel seeds to your next meatball mixture or sprinkle on cooked carrots or winter squash.

- ◉ Lightly toast the seeds and serve them as a garnish for seafood.

Garlic

Garlic, one of the earliest cultivated herbs, is a member of the lily family and close relative of leeks, shallots, and chives. Each bulb of garlic is made up of many sections called cloves. For every pound of garlic planted, five to seven pounds may be harvested. It is a staple in many of the world's cuisines. "Stinking Rose" is the historical name for garlic.

Fun Facts and Folklore

- Ancient cultures regarded garlic as both sacred and strength-enhancing. Early Egyptians fed garlic to the slaves who built their pyramids, while Greeks used it to purify temples. Greek and Roman athletes alike ate garlic before sporting events, and soldiers of that time ate it before going off to war.

- Garlic has long had a reputation for protecting from evil and conferring long life. In 1858, Louis Pasteur discovered it could kill bacteria and recent studies demonstrate that garlic may help reduce blood cholesterol, reduce the risks of infection, and block certain cancers.

- Gilroy, California is known as the "The Garlic Capital of the World." Gilroy Foods processes more garlic than any other factory in the world. Products include pickled, minced, and powdered garlic.

- Garlic contains a strong essential oil which remains in the body long after it is eaten. This affects a person's breath and even skin odor. One of the best ways to neutralize garlic on the breath is to chew a bit of fresh parsley. To remove the smell of garlic from hands, sprinkle them with salt and rinse in cold water.

Try This!

- Whole and uncut garlic adds fragrance to cooking oil or a simmering dish. When sliced, it imparts a stronger flavor, and mincing or pressing adds the most intense flavor to dishes. In other words, the more you do to garlic, the more garlic flavor you will get.

- Try roasting whole garlic cloves with new potatoes or root vegetables, or add a few cloves of garlic to a roasting pan of meat or chicken.

- Another idea is to mince generous amounts of raw garlic and mix with plain yogurt and shredded cucumber to use as a dip for vegetables or chips.

Ginger

Ginger, often referred to as a root, is actually a rhizome. It originated in southern China, and then spread to India, Southeast Asia, West Africa, and the Caribbean. Its name is from the Sanskrit word meaning "with a body like a horn."

Fun Facts and Folklore

- Ginger has been important in Chinese medicine for centuries and is mentioned in the writings of Confucius. It is also named in the Koran, indicating it was known in Arab countries as far back as AD 650. It has been used in Western Europe since the ninth century.

- Ginger was a common trade article in medieval and Renaissance times and was one of the spices used against the plague.

- In England ginger was used mainly as a baking spice and during the fifteenth century, gingerbread became a gift symbolizing love and respect. Elizabeth I had a fancy for gingerbread, which her cooks made into the likenesses of her courtiers. These became the prototype for our traditional gingerbread men.

- In English pubs and taverns during the 1800s, barkeepers put out small containers of ground ginger for people to sprinkle on their beer or ale. This is the origin of ginger ale.

- In the 1980s British researchers found that powdered ginger was twice as effective as Dramamine in preventing motion sickness.

Try This!

- Cut fresh ginger into julienne strips and fry the strips in oil for a crunchy garnish for fish.

- Mix some ground or fresh ginger with chopped lime zest to brush atop grilled fish. Or add to melted butter and use as a basting for roasted or grilled poultry and meats.

- Use crushed gingersnaps as a thickener for gravy, or dried gingerbread crumbs as a breading for meat. Mixed with butter, gingerbread or gingersnap crumbs make a tangy pie crust.

- Finely chopped candied ginger is wonderful atop vanilla ice cream or fresh melon.

Horseradish

Horseradish is a hardy perennial, native to Eastern Europe and western Asia. As a member of the mustard family, its cousins are kale, cauliflower, Brussels sprouts, and radishes. Its large white pungent root is often grated.

Fun Facts and Folklore

- Horseradish has been used through the ages. It is one of the "five bitter herbs" eaten at Passover and was used by early Greeks as a back rub and aphrodisiac. During Europe's Middle Ages it served as a cough expectorant. In the 1600s, horseradish was mixed with wormwood and tansy into an ale for reviving weary travelers.

- By the 1860s, horseradish was available in bottles, making it one of the first convenience condiments.

- Horseradish is still planted and harvested mostly by hand, and today approximately six million gallons of prepared horseradish are produced annually in the United States.

- The International Herb Association named horseradish its 2011 Herb of the Year. Horseradish even has its own website: Horseradish.org.

Try This!

- To liven up the taste of mashed potatoes, add a dollop of paste made from smashed fresh garlic, olive oil, and horseradish.

- You can also mix horseradish with apricot preserves and a little mustard for a good ham glaze.

- Add a bit of horseradish and freshly squeezed lemon juice to bottled chili sauce for a great shrimp cocktail sauce.

- Apple pie filling has a nutty-sweet flavor when freshly grated horseradish is added.

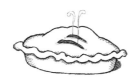

Mace & Nutmeg

The nutmeg tree is the only plant that offers two spices. Nutmeg is the kernel of an apricot-like fruit of the tree. Mace is the thin, leathery tissue between the nut and the fruit pulp. The tree is native to Indonesia and now is also grown extensively in Grenada.

Fun Facts and Folklore

- Legend has it that birds on the islands where nutmeg grows become intoxicated because its aroma is so strong.

- During the Middle Ages, tucking a nutmeg into the left armpit before attending a social event was believed to attract admirers. In eighteenth century England and America, pocket graters were part of the well-dressed person's ensemble, and no trousseau was complete without a hinged container to keep the family nutmeg.

- Connecticut is known as "The Nutmeg State" because slick Yankee peddlers supposedly sold whittled wooden "nutmegs" to unsuspecting housewives.

- Raised commercially, nutmeg is graded by dumping the dried kernels into water. The heaviest sink and are graded highest. The rest are sized through screens. Those that float are used in medicine and cosmetics.

- While the aroma and taste of mace and nutmeg are similar, mace is the more potent of the two. Because each tree produces much less mace than nutmeg, it is also the more expensive spice.

Try This!

- Add flavor to cooked greens, such as kale or spinach, with a few gratings of nutmeg. Cauliflower, cabbage, and all kinds of squash also benefit from the flavor of nutmeg.

- Add ground mace or nutmeg to mashed or sweet potatoes for a comforting side dish.

- You might also add a dash of ground mace to cooked lentils or vegetable stew for additional flavor.

- Include a bit of nutmeg or mace anytime you add walnuts to a dish.

- Try adding a pinch each of nutmeg and thyme to chicken broth, and garnish the soup with a slice of lemon.

Marjoram

Marjoram, a perennial member of the mint family indigenous to the Mediterranean, shares botanical similarities with oregano. In fact, although oregano was long considered "wild marjoram," the plants do not look similar, and marjoram has a milder, sweeter flavor than oregano. Currently ninety percent of the world's supply comes from Egypt.

Fun Facts and Folklore

- Ancient Egyptians used marjoram with other fragrant spices to appease the gods in the embalming process, while ancient Greeks believed that if marjoram grew on a grave, the deceased would enjoy eternal peace and happiness.

Salt, Pepper, & Beyond

- European singers have used marjoram tea sweetened with honey to preserve their voices, and the herb is often used as a steam inhalant to clear the sinuses. A USDA analysis showed that marjoram, along with oregano, has the highest amount of antioxidants of any herb, and even more fresh than dried.

- The floral aroma of marjoram enhances soaps, pomanders, and herbal wreaths.

- Marjoram is easy to grow from seed and thrives in full sun and somewhat dry conditions. Be sure to pinch back the flower buds to keep the plant from getting lanky and going to seed.

Try This!

- Grill a chicken rubbed with garlic, salt, coarse black pepper, and marjoram.

- Chopped fresh marjoram sprinkled liberally on scrambled eggs or cooked carrots, peas, or onions adds a vibrant touch. Or use it as a garnish for split pea soup.

- Mix chopped marjoram into meatloaf or add it to stuffing mixtures for chicken or turkey.

- Softened butter blended with dried marjoram makes a tasty topping for fish.

Mint

Mint, native to the Mediterranean and western Asia, has about thirty species and as many as six hundred varieties. In fact, a ninth century monk proclaimed he would rather "count the sparks in Vulcan's furnace than to count the varieties of mint."

Fun Facts and Folklore

- According to legend, Minthe was a nymph and Pluto's lover. In a rage when she found out, Pluto's wife turned Minthe into a lowly plant. Pluto could not undo the spell, but he softened it by giving her a sweet scent which would perfume the air when her leaves were stepped upon.

- During the fourteenth century, mint was used for whitening the teeth, while today peppermint is often used in liqueurs, toothpastes, soaps, and mouthwashes. It is also used for clearing up stuffy head colds, as a strong digestive aid, and a mild sedative.

- Mice are averse to the smell of mint, either fresh or dried, and will leave any food it is scattered on untouched.

- Growing mint is easy. However, if you do not keep it cut back, it can invade the entire garden. Many varieties propagate by underground runner, so you may need to pull out wandering plants.

Try This!

- Combine spearmint with orange peel in vinegar and use it as a marinade for lamb or as a dressing for spring salads.

- Sprinkle freshly chopped mint on new potatoes or cooked carrots, or add chopped mint leaves to the cooking liquid when preparing cauliflower.

- Do as some Italians do, and add a little chopped mint to your minestrone to give it personality.

- Finely chop mint and incorporate it into softened vanilla ice cream, then top with fresh berries for a scrumptious dessert.

Mustard

This erect herbaceous annual, a relative of broccoli and cabbage, grows well in temperate climates and can reach a height of six feet depending on the variety. The flowers yield fruit pods containing mustard seeds which must be harvested when they are nearly fully developed, but before they burst when ripe. Currently the province of Saskatchewan in Canada provides about half of the world's supply.

Fun Facts and Folklore

- At first, mustard was considered a medicinal plant rather than a cooking ingredient. Hippocrates advised its use for muscular relief, while others prescribed it for scorpion stings, snake bites, toothache, and rheumatism. Mustard plasters are still used today to stimulate the immune system and as a treatment for the common cold.

- Pope John XXII (1316-1334) enjoyed mustard so much that he created a new Vatican position (*grand moutardier du pape* or "mustard-maker to the pope") and appointed his nephew to the post. King Louis XI of France traveled with his own royal mustard pot, just in case his hosts did not serve it. Grey Poupon, anyone?

- Originally the condiment, not the plant, was called mustard. The condiment was made by grinding the seeds of a plant into a paste and mixing it with an unfermented wine called "must."

- Depending on the variety, the seeds may be yellow, brown, or black. Yellow mustard tends to be less pungent and has good preservative qualities, so it is used in pickling and ballpark mustard. Brown seeds are a bit more pungent and are used in pickling and as a main ingredient in European and Chinese mustards. Black mustard seeds have the strongest bite.

- Americans eat more mustard than any other spice except for black pepper.

Try This!

- Try adding a couple of pinches of powdered mustard to salted water when boiling root vegetables such as carrots, parsnips, or potatoes to enhance their flavor.

- A little prepared mustard enhances the flavor of potato and macaroni salads.

- Adding a pinch of powdered mustard to the dry ingredients of chocolate cakes, brownies, and cookies will intensify the chocolatey flavor.

Oregano

Oregano is a perennial herb native to Europe and the Mediterranean region. Oregano is the spice that gives pizza its characteristic flavor and it is often used in chili powder and tomato-based sauces.

Fun Facts and Folklore

- Greeks and Romans regarded oregano as a symbol of joy and happiness, and traditionally brides and grooms were crowned with a laurel of oregano.

- Pliny praised oregano's medicinal uses, from strengthening the stomach to curing headaches and nervousness. The leaves provided reddish brown dyes for early linens, and smokers used its dried leaves as tobacco.

- Although used in Europe since the Middle Ages, oregano was hardly known in the United States until the twentieth century, when GIs returning from Italy brought word of this fragrant herb back to the United States. Sales of oregano actually increased by 5200 percent between 1948 and 1956 due to "pizza mania."

- Currently, oregano's biggest commercial use is in perfumes.

- Depending on climate, oregano grows as either a perennial or an annual plant. As a perennial, it needs warm, sunny days. If you cut back a mature plant to the ground, the plant will develop more stems and become fuller.

Try This!

- Try tossing fresh oregano leaves into your next salad.

- Sauté aromatic vegetables, such as onions, carrots, or celery, in olive oil with some garlic and dried or chopped fresh oregano.

- Add a pinch of oregano to mushroom, bean, or cheese recipes.

- Add a unique addition to a buffet table with a salad composed of chopped olives, chopped fresh oregano, diced pimiento, and grated carrot, all dressed with a little olive oil.

Paprika

❖

Paprika is a spice which comes from a mild red pepper. Indigenous to the Western Hemisphere, much of the commercial pepper cultivation for paprika is now in Hungary and Spain. One of the newer spices, paprika did not appear on the culinary scene until the 1700s.

Fun Facts and Folklore

- Hungary was the first country to use the zesty red powder. They saw it as a perfect spice, with color, fragrance, and flavor. Unrivaled in the world today, Hungarian paprika labeled from the Szeged region is strictly controlled by the Hungarian Ministry of Agriculture.

- Paprika has ingrained itself in the Hungarian national spirit and *Paprika Janesi* (Johnny Paprika) is a traditional figure in the Hungarian Punch and Judy shows and village fairs.

- Pound for pound, paprika has a higher Vitamin C content than citrus fruit and more carotene than carrots. It actually stimulates blood circulation. The Hungarian scientist Dr. Szent-Gyorgyi won the Nobel Prize for research on the vitamin content of paprika.

- Although paprika can range from mild to hot, most commercially available paprika is mild, or "sweet." Some specialty food stores also carry hot paprika, made spicier with the seeds and stems of the pepper fruit, and smoked paprika, which adds a distinctive flavor to foods.

- Commercial food manufacturers use paprika to add color. When you find a red-orange or red-brown manufactured food item, check the label. If the label lists "natural color," paprika is the likely ingredient.

Try This!

- To season cooked broccoli or cauliflower, lightly sauté chopped cloves of garlic, a small amount of sweet paprika, and a bay leaf in a little extra virgin olive oil. Remove the bay leaf, add a splash of wine vinegar and some chopped red onion, then pour the mixture over the vegetables.

- A dusting of sweet paprika on deviled eggs or potato salad adds an eye-pleasing appearance. Also consider sprinkling paprika on cream sauces, cheese sauces, or cucumbers.

- Paprika goes well with all kinds of mushrooms.

Parsley

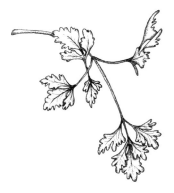

Native to the Mediterranean region, parsley is a bright green biennial herb with a faint peppery tang. Although there are more than thirty varieties, the two most popular forms are curly leaf and Italian flat leaf.

Fun Facts and Folklore

- Ancient Greeks thought parsley was sacred and used it to adorn victors of the Isthmian sports games, to feed their horses before battle to ensure valor, and to decorate tombs of the deceased.

- As far back as the time of Hippocrates, parsley was used as a medicinal cure-all. Gentlemen of the time wore garlands of parsley to protect themselves from drunkenness.

- Another early use was cosmetic. People believed that powdering your head with parsley seed three nights every year ensured that you would never lose your hair.

- In times past, a sprig of parsley on your plate at a restaurant signified that the master chef had personally attended to your order.

- Curly parsley works as an antidote for garlic. Eat a sprig of parsley after a garlicky meal or vigorously rub fresh parsley leaves on your fingers after you have handled garlic.

Try This!

- Chopped parsley leaves add a fresh taste to sauces, soups, and stuffings.

- Use the leaves as part of your salad greens, or chop leaves over vegetables.

- You can also fry parsley leaves in olive oil for an unusual garnish.

- Freeze parsley stems to use when making stock.

- Pierce a beef roast all over with a sharp knife and stuff the knife slits with parsley leaves.

Poppy Seeds

Poppy seeds are tiny, nutty-tasting, blue-gray seeds found inside the opium plant. Opium is native to the Mediterranean, India, China, Turkey, and Iran. Holland and Canada are currently the largest producers of commercial poppy seeds.

Fun Facts and Folklore

- The plant's species name means 'sleep inducing,' and its narcotic effect has provided much incentive for cultivation through the centuries. However, western poppies grown for their seeds have none of the alkaloids that comprise the narcotic.

- Egyptians cultivated poppies for cooking oil as early as 1500 BC and the poppy was probably one of the earliest plants cultivated in Europe. The red poppy flower has been the symbol of fallen warriors throughout history and was adopted as an emblem to commemorate Veterans Day in the United States.

• Today various ethnic cuisines use poppy seeds in a variety of ways. In European and Mideastern cooking, the seeds flavor breads, cakes, rolls, and cookies. In Turkey, the seeds are often ground and used in desserts. In India, the ground seeds thicken sauces, while in Jewish, German, and Slavic cooking the poppy seeds flavor noodle, fish, and vegetable dishes.

Try This!

- Try adding poppy seeds to buttered egg noodles, potatoes, or fruit salad dressings.

- Toast white poppy seeds along with chopped nuts such as cashews or walnuts and add the mixture to cooked lentils, rice, or a stuffing mix.

- Consider using poppy seeds as part of a light coating when sautéing meat patties.

- Add poppy seeds to vegetable stir-frys and stewed vegetable mixtures, or sprinkle toasted poppy seeds over coleslaw.

> To ensure freshness, check spices annually. Crush a small amount of a spice in your hand, sniffing for rich, full aroma.

Rosemary

Rosemary is a spiky, evergreen member of the mint family with a robust taste and scent similar to pine. It is native to the Mediterranean and is now widely grown in temperate climates.

Fun Facts and Folklore

- In Latin rosemary means "dew of the sea." References to rosemary can be found written in cuneiform on stone tablets dating from the fifth millennium BC.

- Early Greek students wove rosemary through their hair to stimulate their memory during exams.

- For centuries, rosemary has been a symbol of friendship and faithfulness. Early Romans wove rosemary into bridal wreaths and put it under nuptial mattresses to encourage faithfulness, as well as to keep insects and mildew away.

- Folklore has it that if rosemary grows vigorously in a family's garden, it means a woman heads the household. In fact, it was suspected that some lords in Gloucestershire and other English counties would privately injure growing rosemary in order to destroy this evidence of their lack of authority.

Try This!

- Combine crushed rosemary leaves with olive oil as a flavoring for squash, mushrooms, and potatoes. Or chop fresh rosemary with melted butter and a pinch of salt to season red potatoes and other vegetables.

- Soak a few sprigs of rosemary in water and toss them on glowing charcoal during grilling, or make a unique skewer for kabobs by stripping rosemary stems of their leaves.

- Stuff a chicken with cut-up lemons and a few rosemary sprigs.

- Try adding a long stem of rosemary to a pitcher of iced tea. Very refreshing!

Saffron

Saffron is actually the dried stigma of a small purple crocus native to Western Asia. It is now cultivated primarily in India, Turkey, Spain, and Iran.

Fun Facts and Folklore

- More than 75,000 crocuses are needed to produce a pound of saffron. Because propagation depends on human intervention and the stigmas must be hand-picked from each flower, saffron is the world's most expensive spice.

- In ancient times, saffron was used in medicines, food, perfume making, and dyes. Ancient Greeks and Romans scattered saffron to perfume public baths. The red-gold threads were highly prized by pharaohs and kings as an aphrodisiac, yet large amounts of this spice produce deathly narcotic effects.

- The word saffron comes from an Arab word meaning yellow. The followers of the Buddha selected the saffron as the official color of their priesthood shortly after his death and "donning the saffron robes" has come to mean becoming a Buddhist monk.

- Because it has always been expensive, saffron has long been open to adulteration. Pliny wrote that it was the most frequently falsified commodity in ancient Rome. In the Middle Ages, punishment for this crime could be extreme. In fact, in the 1400s, a German was ordered burned at the stake for adulterating saffron.

Try This!

- ☺ Try steeping a pinch of crushed saffron strands in a little hot water for fifteen to twenty minutes and adding the mixture to a chicken stew or to the cooking liquid for rice, risotto, or even vegetables. Remember a little goes a long way to add flavor and color.

- ☺ Make saffron butter by toasting saffron threads and finely pulverizing them with a little salt before mixing them into softened butter. Baste butter on fish as you bake or broil it.

- ☺ Add a few crushed strands of saffron to simple syrup (sugar and water) and use it as a poaching medium for fresh fruit.

Red spices will gradually turn brown in color as they age.

Sage

Sage, a member of the mint family, is an evergreen shrub that grows throughout the world wherever there is good drainage and full sun. There are about five hundred varieties of sage and the best sage now comes from the Dalmatian region of Yugoslavia.

Fun Facts and Folklore

- Sage was revered as a medicinal plant by the Greeks and Romans and regular consumption was supposed to give an even disposition to those with excitable natures and a healthy old age to everyone. It was recommended to older persons because it was believed to restore failing memory and banish melancholy and depression.

- Arab physicians in the twelfth century went so far as to claim that sage extended life by causing the lamp of life to burn brightly almost to the point of immortality.

- With its aromatic oils, sage is frequently used in making soaps and perfumes. Native Americans use the bound stems of sage as smudge sticks for spiritual purification ceremonies.

- Unlike most herbs, the flavor in sage leaves intensifies as they dry. Throughout the ages the leaves have been brewed into tea.

Try This!

- Sage matches well with fat-rich foods such as duck, as its properties are believed to aid digestion.

- Try rubbing a combination of sage, cracked pepper, and garlic into pork tenderloin or pork chops before cooking.

- Add sage to pasta sauces, tomato-based soups, and bean salads.

- The next time you prepare a bacon, lettuce, and tomato sandwich, try adding a few fresh sage leaves.

- Many varieties of sage can enhance the flavor of fruit salad. Taste a leaf to decide, and use it finely chopped within the salad mixture or whole for a garnish.

- Consider using sage leaves as an edible garnish on a cheese platter.

Savory

Savory is a low-growing annual native to warm temperate regions of the Northern Hemisphere and found in dry, sunny areas world-wide.

Fun Facts and Folklore

- In the first century BC, Virgil grew savory as ambrosia for his bees because of way it flavored honey. Early Romans used savory in vinegar as one of their main condiments on account of its peppery taste.

- The original name for San Francisco was Yerba Buena, which means good herb. Yerba Buena is actually a variety of savory, and early settlers dried the herb and drank it as a tea to cure a variety of ailments.

- Today savory is commonly used as an ingredient in toothpaste and soaps because of its pungent oils.

- The German word for this herb is *Bohenkraut*, which means "bean herb." Savory naturally aids the digestion of sometimes problematic legumes.

Try This!

- Most commonly, savory is added to various legumes or mixed with other herbs as a general seasoning for stews, stuffing, and sauces.

- Try including savory in meatloaf and hamburgers, or add some to biscuits or as seasoning for chicken pie.

- Scrambled eggs and peas perk up with the addition of chopped savory.

- Add a pinch of dried savory or several pinches of chopped fresh leaves to tomato soup, three-bean salad, succotash, or a pot of beans or lentils.

- Infuse the liquid of stewed fruits with a half teaspoon of dried savory.

Dried herbs are stronger than fresh herbs so use less. One teaspoon dried is equal to two to three teaspoons fresh.

Sesame Seeds

Sesame is an annual plant, growing up to six feet tall, with oblong leaves and seed pods. The seeds contain over thirty-five percent protein and are also high in vitamin D. They have a nutty aroma and a buttery taste. Most of the four billion pounds of seeds produced annually are pressed into oil which, unlike the seeds themselves, is exceptionally resistant to rancidity.

Fun Facts and Folklore

- There are many recorded uses of sesame seeds throughout history. Over five thousand years ago, the Chinese burned sesame oil as a light source and as soot for their ink-blocks. As early as 1550 BC, Egyptians used sesame seeds as medicine. Ancient Greek soldiers carried sesame seeds as energy boosting rations, while the Romans made a kind of hummus from sesame seeds and cumin.

- According to Assyrian legend, the gods drank wine made from sesame seeds the night before they created the earth. In early Hindu legends, sesame seeds represented immortality.

- Harvesting sesame seeds is tricky, as the capsule that holds the seeds shatters when ripe. The phrase "open sesame" from *Ali Baba and the Forty Thieves* refers to the sound sesame seeds make when they literally pop from the ripe pod at the slightest touch.

Try This!

- The nutty flavor of sesame seeds is enhanced by toasting them until lightly browned in a small dry skillet or a 350°F oven.

- Try adding a tablespoon of toasted sesame seeds to a cup of bread crumbs and using the mixture to coat chicken breasts or pork chops before frying.

- Vegetables such as green beans, broccoli, and roasted asparagus benefit from a sprinkle of the toasted seeds.

- Toasted sesame seeds add crunchy goodness to noodle dishes.

- Fish fillets also get added crunch when they are moistened with teriyaki or soy sauce, sprinkled with sesame seeds, then broiled.

Star Anise

Star Anise is the hard, star-shaped fruit of a small evergreen tree native to southwest China.

Fun Facts and Folklore

- Star anise is one of the traditional ingredients of five-spice powder in Chinese cooking and is widely used in Indian and Vietnamese cuisine as well.

- Star anise is also the source of a primary ingredient used to create an anti-flu drug. In fact, in 2005 there was a temporary shortage of star anise due to its use in drug making.

- Traditional Chinese medicine uses star anise to assist in relieving cold stagnation. It has also been used in tea to alleviate the pains of rheumatism and chewed after meals to assist digestion.

Try This!

◎ Whole star anises can be added to stews, broths, soups, and braising liquids to intensify the flavors, especially in pork and chicken dishes.

◎ Consider using a whole star anise as a garnish for cream soups, poached fish, or fruit cups. Diners can nibble on the star at the end of the meal as both digestive and breath sweetener.

◎ Star anise can give a nice kick to cranberry and apple sauces.

◎ When poaching pears, add one or two stars to the liquid.

◎ Consider adding star anise segments to your smoker chip mix when smoking fish or poultry.

◎ Flavor carrots, parsnips, and squash with ground star anise.

When reducing sugar, use sweet spices such as star anise, cinnamon, or nutmeg. These spices give the impression of greater sweetness.

Tarragon

Tarragon is called "King of Herbs" by the French, who use it as the main flavoring in many of their sauces. It is a small, shrubby herb in the sunflower family, native to southern Russia and western Asia. Its leaves have a fresh, licorice-like flavor.

Fun Facts and Folklore

- Tarragon root was used by the ancient Greeks as a remedy for toothaches.

- People in the Middle Ages believed that tarragon could ward off serpents and dragons, and, more practically, heal snake bites.

- In England the Tudor family introduced tarragon into the royal gardens in the late 1500s, and it became popular as a cooked vegetable. In India it was combined with fennel to produce a drink held precious by the royals.

- Tarragon does not produce true seeds, and so must be grown from root cuttings. Gardeners know that if tarragon is not divided regularly, it will actually strangle itself.

Try This!

- Blend tarragon with butter, chives, and lemon as a baste for chicken, fish, or seafood.

- Make tarragon-flavored vinegar by putting freshly-gathered leaves into a wide-mouthed jar and covering with good white vinegar. After letting it stand several hours, strain the vinegar and cork the bottle.

- Add tarragon leaves to your salad greens or mince fresh leaves as a garnish and flavoring for egg dishes.

- Sprinkle finely chopped tarragon on gravies, lentils, or rice.

- Try adding tarragon leaves to a bowl of orange segments for a light, healthy dessert.

❖

Salt, Pepper, & Beyond

Add fresh herbs at the end of cooking to preserve their color and flavor.

Thyme

A low-growing shrub and member of the mint family, thyme is indigenous to the Mediterranean. There are over sixty varieties of thyme, and although all thyme varieties are nectar sources, the wild thyme of Greece creates much sought-after honey.

Fun Facts and Folklore

- The word "thyme" in Greek comes from *thymon*, meaning courage.

- Early Athenians used thyme in the kitchen, made liqueurs with it, burned it in their temples, and bathed in it. In fact, it was a part of every gentleman's toilet kit. To say one "smelled of thyme" in ancient Athens was considered high praise.

- Believing that thyme built courage, Romans bathed in thyme-scented waters to prepare for battle, and Scottish highlanders prepared tea of wild thyme for the same purpose. European ladies of the Middle Ages embroidered a sprig of thyme on tunics and scarves for their knights, again for courage.

- During Renaissance times, Spaniards and Italians grazed sheep and goats on thyme for the flavor it gave their meat.

Try This!

- Include thyme in your rub and marinade mixtures for chicken and pork.

- When slow cooking beef and chicken, add one or two sprigs of fresh thyme.

- Sauté sliced mushrooms in butter and thyme to bring out their earthy flavor.

- Cheese and egg dishes, poultry stuffing, and spaghetti and pizza sauces are enhanced by a small amount of freshly chopped thyme or a dash of ground thyme.

- Thyme flowers may be used as a garnish or scattered in a salad mix.

Turmeric

Turmeric is a member of the ginger family and native to Southeast Asia. It is widely available and thus is one of the least expensive spices. It has a pungent taste and a yellow-orange color.

Fun Facts and Folklore

- Since antiquity, turmeric has been used both as a dye and as a condiment. Now it is widely used as a food coloring and as one of the principle ingredients in curry powder. It also gives ballpark mustard its bright yellow color.

- Turmeric has long been used in both Ayurvedic and Chinese medicine as an anti-inflammatory agent. It is also used to treat digestive disorders and liver problems, and to heal skin diseases and wounds.

- Although it does not have the same flavor, turmeric is often substituted for the much more expensive saffron.

- Turmeric is used in rituals of the Hindu religion. Many Indonesian bridal couples color their arms with it for the wedding ceremony. In Malaysia, some women coat the skin on their stomachs with turmeric after childbirth.

Try This!

- ◉ Stir a small amount of turmeric into sour cream for a lush dressing for cold shellfish.

- ◉ Add a pinch of turmeric to fish soup, or blend with melted butter and drizzle it over cooked vegetables.

- ◉ Add ground turmeric to your rubs for chicken or beef, or include it in the cooking liquid for rice or couscous.

- ◉ A bit of ground turmeric blended in coconut milk imparts additional flavor and color to soups and seafood dishes.

To become familiar with a particular spice or herb, mix a bit into butter or cream cheese and let it stand for about an hour. Spread on a cracker and taste.

Vanilla

Vanilla comes from the ripe seed pod of a member of the orchid family native to Mexico. In the wild, the perennial creeping vine can extend as long as eighty feet.

Fun Facts and Folklore

- Both the Mayans and the Aztecs used vanilla as part of a royal drink by mixing it with water, spices, cocoa beans, and honey. After the explorer Cortez observed the Aztec King Montezuma drinking the concoction, he brought vanilla beans back to Europe. European nobility used it to flavor drinking chocolate.

- Until a way to hand pollinate the blossoms was discovered in the 1830s, Mexico had a complete monopoly on vanilla production. The melipone bee and a few types of hummingbirds that live exclusively in that region were the only pollinators. Now growers use a pointed bamboo stick resembling a feather duster to pollinate the blossoms, so vanilla can be produced in other tropical regions of the world.

- Vanilla is one of the world's most expensive spices because production is so labor-intensive. Hand pollination and harvesting, followed by nearly six months of curing involving alternately sweating and drying the green pods until they become slightly wrinkled, moist, fragrant, and a rich brown-black color is required. Five pounds of green pods will reduce to one pound of dried pods ready for market.

- The thousands of seeds in a single pod can flavor a few gallons of ice cream.

Try This!

- Beware of imitation or vanilla "flavor" products, as one ingredient is waste paper pulp!

- Try using a hint of pure vanilla extract to deepen the flavor of mashed sweet potatoes or squash, or mix with a bit of butter as a glaze for carrots.

- Enhance your ham glaze with a bit of vanilla extract, or make a vanilla-flavored cream sauce to top grilled chicken breasts.

- Vanilla pods themselves, when rinsed and dried, can be chopped and put in a container of sugar. Within weeks the vanilla sugar can be used for baking or sweetening coffee and tea. Or mix a little of the sugar into cream and use it atop fresh or stewed fruit.

- Add a dash of pure vanilla extract to any rum drink.

Especially Tasty Recipes

A Tribute to
M.A.

I was fortunate – although my waistline may not agree – to grow up in a food-loving family. My mother was a gourmet cook, and she spent hours preparing and perfecting exotic dishes for gourmet dinner groups, where the only rule was that the recipe was new to the cook. The rest of the time she experimented on us. We had meals with escargots, calf's tongue, celeriac, tagine, oysters, and quince jelly (though happily not all at the same time). I remember being the only child in school, besides my sisters, with tuna sandwiches made with olives, capers, and herbed mayonnaise on stone-ground wheat bread. Of course, back then, far from being thrilled, we desperately wanted the kind of "normal" sandwich – tuna, Best Foods mayo, and Wonder bread – the other kids would trade us for!

As we got older my mother encouraged us – or, well, insisted – that we participate in meal preparation, starting with Christmas cookies and salad dressings and progressing to full meals. Fortunately she felt strongly enough about our education (and about having help cooking for a family of six) to overlook the not-so-occasional kitchen mess. As much as I may have grumbled about being in the kitchen then, I am grateful now for my mother's enthusiasm and patience, and for her broadening of my culinary horizons. Sadly M.A. is no longer with us, but her legacy lives on. Many of the recipes that follow are her favorites. Others are my own creation … but I suspect she would approve.

Chef's Notes

You will notice as you read through this recipe collection that there are relatively few entrees and a preponderance of sides and sauces. That is because I believe the easiest way to incorporate flavor into your meals is to add a simple rub, marinade, or compound butter to your existing protein, include a tasty side or two, and voilà – deliciousness. And although I am as much a fan of gooey desserts as the next person, if I can satisfy my sweet tooth with a fruit-based dessert, all the better for my heart and hips. That said, I am afraid I could not resist including my favorite chocolate mousse recipe …

Although the recipes are (mostly) simple to prepare, they do presume a certain familiarity with basic cooking techniques. If you are a novice cook who would like to learn, say, the difference between "diced" and "julienned," I encourage you to refer to the Resources section at the end of the book.

The recipes that follow are designed to serve four. If you are serving more (or you are really hungry), plan on doubling the recipe; if you are feeding fewer, you can cut most of the recipes in half, or use the extra as leftovers. Don't be surprised, though, if you have nothing left.

Enjoy!

A quick caveat on salt and pepper in these recipes: Quantities are included to give a novice cook some idea of what might be appropriate in a given recipe. Please use them as guidelines only, and remember that all seasonings should be added "to taste." Use more or less as your palate dictates.

Starters

❖ Green Goddess Dip ❖

This fresh dip is terrific with raw vegetables, cooked shrimp, and artichokes. You can also replace the mayonnaise and sour cream with equal parts buttermilk and low-fat milk for a refreshing salad dressing. It makes a generous cup and a half.

½ cup mayonnaise
½ cup light sour cream
¼ cup chopped scallion
2 tablespoons chopped fresh chives
2 tablespoons chopped fresh parsley

2 tablespoons chopped fresh tarragon
2 tablespoons chopped fresh chervil
1 tablespoon anchovy paste
2 tablespoons fresh lemon juice
Kosher salt and pepper to taste

Combine all ingredients in a food processor and process until smooth.

❖ Sun-Dried Tomato Pesto Dip ❖

This dip makes about two cups. I warn you in advance, it is addictive …

½ cup sun-dried tomatoes in oil,
   drained
12 cherry tomatoes, halved
1 cup fresh basil leaves
2 tablespoons pine nuts, toasted

1 garlic clove, minced
¼ cup balsamic vinegar
1½ tablespoons granulated sugar
1 tablespoon olive oil
1½ teaspoons kosher salt

In a food processor, pulse sun-dried tomatoes, cherry tomatoes, basil leaves, pine nuts, and garlic until finely chopped. Add remaining ingredients and process until almost smooth. Serve with vegetable sticks, crostini, or tortilla chips.

❖ Cheddar-Chutney Spread ❖

This spread has been my family's "go-to" appetizer for as long as I can remember. (And that's a while!) Although it has three steps, each is simple and can be prepared in advance. Serve with baguette slices or crisp sesame wafers.

4 ounces sharp cheddar, shredded
6 ounces cream cheese, softened
3 tablespoons dry sherry
¾ teaspoon mild curry powder *

Kosher salt and pepper to taste
½ cup mango chutney,
preferably Major Greys
1 bunch scallions, minced

In a food processor, combine cheddar cheese, cream cheese, sherry, curry, salt, and pepper; process until smooth. Turn into a shallow flat-bottomed dish, smoothing top, and chill until firm, at least 20 minutes. At serving time, chop chutney and spread it over cheese mixture; top with minced scallions.

Salt, Pepper, & Beyond

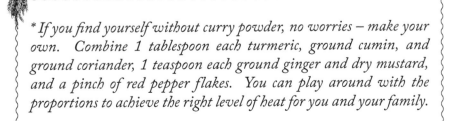

If you find yourself without curry powder, no worries — make your own. Combine 1 tablespoon each turmeric, ground cumin, and ground coriander, 1 teaspoon each ground ginger and dry mustard, and a pinch of red pepper flakes. You can play around with the proportions to achieve the right level of heat for you and your family.

❖ Bell Pepper & Goat Cheese Spread ❖

The intriguing flavors of this spread will keep your guests coming back for more. Use any color bell pepper, and serve with toasted pita rounds or other crackers.

2 tablespoons olive oil
1 bell pepper, diced
4 garlic cloves, chopped
2 teaspoons chopped fresh rosemary
½ teaspoon ground coriander

¼ teaspoon ground fennel seeds
¼ teaspoon ground black pepper
¼ teaspoon dried thyme
1 bay leaf
½ teaspoon kosher salt

6 ounces goat cheese, softened

In a medium skillet, sauté bell peppers in olive oil until tender, about 5 minutes. Add garlic, rosemary, coriander, fennel, black pepper, thyme, and bay leaf; simmer 5 minutes. Cool to room temperature; season with salt. Remove bay leaf and transfer to food processor along with goat cheese; process until smooth.

❖ Cit's Cauliflower Popcorn ❖

My sister Cit, a great chef in her own right, graciously offers this excellent alternative to the more traditional fat-laden Super Bowl or World Series fare.

1 head cauliflower
1 teaspoon mild curry powder

½ teaspoon kosher salt
3 tablespoons olive oil

Preheat oven to 425°F. Cut cauliflower into bite-sized florets. Add curry and salt, tossing to coat. Add olive oil and toss to coat again. Spread cauliflower in a single layer on a half-sheet pan, leaving space between florets. Roast in middle of oven for 30 to 40 minutes, turning pieces every 15 minutes, until florets turn golden brown. Transfer to a popcorn bag or bowl and serve at once.

❖ Salmon Ceviche ❖

Enjoy the burst of flavor capers give to the following ceviche. This recipe makes a wonderful starter or light entree. I have to say we like it so much we have it at least once a week as a light supper. If you are also so inclined, double the recipe.

1 (6-ounce) salmon fillet	1 teaspoon minced fresh jalapeño
Juice of 2 limes	1 tablespoon drained capers
1 tablespoon olive oil	1 teaspoon green peppercorns
1½ teaspoons soy sauce	in brine, drained
1 tablespoon minced shallot	Freshly ground black pepper

Slice salmon very thinly across grain and arrange decoratively in a shallow serving dish. Pour lime juice over fillet slices and refrigerate for 10 to 30 minutes. Just before serving, remove from refrigerator and drizzle with olive oil and soy sauce. Top with shallot, jalapeño, capers, and green peppercorns. Finish with a few twists of freshly ground black pepper. Serve with water crackers, pita chips, or toast points.

Entrees

❖ Chicken Dijon ❖

This entrée is much more refined than its ease would lead you to believe. With Rice Pilaf and Broccoli with Basil Sauce, it is a great dish for company. For a weeknight meal, add a quick salad of greens and herbs or steamed vegetables and you are ready to serve.

4 boneless, skinless chicken breast halves
1 teaspoon kosher salt
½ teaspoon ground black pepper
3 tablespoons minced shallots
2 tablespoons butter or olive oil

1 cup white wine
½ teaspoon dried tarragon
1 small bay leaf
2 tablespoons Dijon mustard
½ cup sour cream or yogurt
Pinch of cayenne

Sprinkle chicken breasts with salt and pepper. In a large skillet, sauté shallots in butter or olive oil over moderately high heat until softened. Add chicken breasts and brown on both sides. Reduce heat to low, add wine, tarragon, and bay leaf. Cover and simmer until chicken is tender, about 20 minutes. Transfer chicken to heated platter and keep warm. Raise heat to moderately high and boil liquid until reduced to ½ cup. Discard bay leaf. Whisk in mustard and cook for a few minutes. Reduce heat to low and whisk in sour cream and cayenne. Heat just to boiling and pour over chicken. If desired, garnish with fresh tarragon. Serve at once.

❖ Roasted Chicken Paprika ❖

Save time on a busy weeknight with this easy and delicious chicken recipe.

¼ cup olive oil
1 tablespoon minced shallot
1 garlic clove, minced
Finely grated zest of 1 lemon

1 tablespoon fresh lemon juice
1 tablespoon sweet paprika
1 teaspoon kosher salt
½ teaspoon dried thyme

4 chicken legs and 4 chicken thighs

Preheat oven to 375°F. Combine olive oil, shallot, garlic, lemon zest, lemon juice, paprika, salt, and thyme. Rub oil mixture all over chicken, and refrigerate, covered, for at least 30 minutes. Roast until chicken is tender and skin is crisp. Serve at once.

❖ Horseradish-Crusted Salmon Fillets ❖

Here is an incredibly simple yet elegant way to elevate salmon or other fish fillets from humdrum to sublime.

4 (¾-inch thick) salmon fillets
4 tablespoons butter, softened
3 tablespoons prepared horseradish
1½ cups fresh bread crumbs

1 shallot, minced
Finely grated zest of 1 lemon
Kosher salt and pepper to taste
1½ tablespoons olive oil

In a food processor, pulse together butter, horseradish, bread crumbs, shallot, and lemon zest. Season salmon with salt and pepper. Mound horseradish mixture on top of salmon and press down to cover top. In an oven-proof skillet, heat oil; sauté fillets over medium high heat, horseradish side up, until browned on bottom, 7 to 10 minutes. Place skillet under broiler and broil 3 to 4 minutes or until golden brown on top. Serve at once.

❖ Fish Tacos ❖

The ingredient list for these delicious fish tacos is long, but buy the spices once and you will reach for them again and again. Rest assured, once you have assembled the ingredients, both marinade and tacos go together quickly.

Marinade:
¼ cup olive oil
¼ cup fresh lime juice
¼ cup chopped fresh cilantro
1 teaspoon minced fresh jalapeño
1 garlic clove, minced
1½ teaspoons dried oregano
1½ teaspoons kosher salt
1 teaspoon ancho chile powder
1 teaspoon chipotle chile powder
½ teaspoon ground cumin

Tacos:
4 (½-inch thick) firm white fish fillets
fillets such as tilapia or halibut
1 cup fresh or frozen white corn
12 corn tortillas
¼ cup sour cream
2 avocados, sliced,
sprinkled with lime juice
1 cup shredded green or
red cabbage
2 limes, cut into quarters

Whisk together marinade ingredients. Reserve ½ cup of marinade. In a shallow bowl, pour remaining marinade over fish. Let marinate, refrigerated, for at least 10 minutes. If using fresh corn, cut kernels from cobs. While fillets are marinating, sauté kernels in a dry sauté pan over moderate heat until browned.

Grill fillets over hot coals about 5 minutes per side, or in a panini press for about 5 minutes total, until just firm to the touch. While fillets are grilling, lightly toast tortillas in a dry pan or over a gas flame, and keep them warm in a clean kitchen towel. Stir sour cream into reserved marinade. Slice fillets into bite-sized pieces, place in tortillas, and top with roasted corn, avocado, cabbage, and sour cream sauce. Garnish with lime wedges.

❖ Orange Pork Chops ❖

Serve with Garlic Sage Mashed Potatoes to sop up the yummy sauce.

4 (¾-inch) boneless pork loin chops	2 tablespoons minced shallot
1 teaspoon kosher salt	1 teaspoon ground ginger
½ teaspoon ground pepper	¾ teaspoon fennel seeds
1 tablespoon canola oil	4 orange slices
⅓ cup orange juice	½ cup sour cream

Season pork chops with salt and pepper. Sauté chops in canola oil over moderately high heat until well browned. Reduce heat to medium low. Add orange juice, shallot, ginger, and fennel seeds; cover and simmer 10 minutes. Top each chop with an orange slice; cover and simmer 15 minutes more, or until meat is tender. Transfer orange-topped chops to a serving dish and keep warm. Reduce pan juices over moderately high heat to 2 tablespoons; stir in sour cream, heat through, and pour over chops. Serve at once.

Salt, Pepper, & Beyond

❖ Amazing Pot Roast ❖

Although this pot roast is definitely not designed for a last-minute supper, it is easy and absolutely delicious – perfect for Sunday dinner.

1 (3-pound) boneless beef chuck roast	1 cup beef stock
2 tablespoons all-purpose flour	1 bay leaf
1 teaspoon kosher salt	1 whole star anise
1 teaspoon ground black pepper	2 garlic cloves, minced
2 tablespoons olive oil	1 teaspoon ground ginger
1 onion, finely chopped	1 teaspoon dried dill
2 large carrots, finely chopped	1 teaspoon dried thyme

1 ounce unsweetened chocolate, chopped

Sprinkle roast with flour, salt, and pepper. In Dutch oven, brown all sides of roast in olive oil over moderately high heat. Reduce heat to low and add onions and carrots; cover and cook 10 minutes. Reduce heat to very low and add stock, scraping up browned bits on bottom of pan. Add bay leaf, star anise, garlic, ginger, dill, thyme, and chocolate. Cook, covered, for 3 hours, or until very tender, turning roast occasionally and adding additional stock or water as necessary.

Transfer roast to a serving platter and keep warm. Reduce pan juices over moderately high heat until slightly thickened, about 8 minutes. Pour pan juices over roast or pass separately in a gravy boat. Roast can be sliced in the kitchen or at the table.

❖ Spinach Meatloaf ❖

Just think, with this meatloaf you may be able to get skeptical children (or partners) to eat their vegetables without even noticing. An additional plus is that the meatloaf makes great sandwiches the next day. Feel free to substitute ground pork, lamb, or chicken (or a combination) for the beef.

1½ pounds fresh spinach, wilted, or
2 (10-ounce) frozen spinach, thawed
2 pounds ground beef
1 onion, chopped
¾ teaspoon ground nutmeg

¼ teaspoon ground cinnamon
2 teaspoons kosher salt
¼ teaspoon ground black pepper
3 eggs, lightly beaten
6 strips of bacon

Preheat oven to 350°F. Chop spinach finely and squeeze dry with paper towels. Mix with ground beef, onion, nutmeg, cinnamon, salt, and pepper to taste. Stir in eggs. Form into loaf, place in loaf pan, and arrange bacon strips on top.

Bake meatloaf for 1 hour until firm. Let stand for 10 to 15 minutes before slicing. Serve with Winter Tomato Sauce, or if you are pressed for time, ketchup.

❖ Pasta Bolognese ❖

Rich, hearty – what else can I say? Pass around some fresh grated parmesan.

8 ounces pancetta, chopped
1 onion, chopped
½ cup chopped carrots
½ cup chopped celery
3 garlic cloves, minced
8 ounces ground veal
8 ounces ground beef
½ cup red wine

½ cup beef broth
1 (14-ounce) can diced tomatoes
1 tablespoon tomato paste
1 bay leaf
1 tablespoon minced fresh basil
1 tablespoon minced fresh parsley
½ teaspoon ground allspice
1 teaspoon each kosher salt and pepper

1 pound pasta of your choice

In a large pot, cook pancetta over moderate heat until it releases its fat, about 8 minutes. Add onion, carrots, celery, and garlic; sauté 5 minutes. Add veal and beef and brown well. Reduce heat and stir in wine, broth, tomatoes with their juice, tomato paste, bay leaf, basil, parsley, allspice, salt, and pepper. Simmer about 45 minutes, or until sauce is thickened. Towards end of cooking time, in a large pot of salted boiling water, cook pasta according to package directions; drain. Add pasta to sauce, tossing to coat. Serve at once.

❖ Mediterranean Pasta ❖

This quick pasta recipe is very flexible. Use your favorite kind of pasta, fresh or dried; vary the herbs; sauté additional vegetables, such as sliced carrots or zucchini, along with the shallot and garlic; replace sun-dried tomatoes with fresh, or arugula with spinach. The results will be equally tasty.

12 ounces pasta of your choice
¼ cup olive oil, divided
1 large shallot, minced
2 garlic cloves, minced
4 sun-dried tomatoes in oil,
  drained and julienned
¼ cup pitted Kalamata olives,
  coarsely chopped
2 tablespoons capers

¼ teaspoon red pepper flakes
½ teaspoon dried oregano
1 anchovy fillet, minced
Finely grated zest of 1 lemon
¼ cup minced fresh parsley
2 cups fresh arugula
Kosher salt and pepper to taste
2 tablespoons fresh lemon juice
½ cup fresh grated parmesan

Cook pasta according to package directions. Drain, reserving ¾ cup of cooking liquid. While pasta is cooking, in a large skillet heat 1 tablespoon of olive oil over medium heat. Add shallot, garlic, sun-dried tomatoes, olives, capers, pepper flakes, and oregano, and cook, stirring, for 3 minutes until shallot is tender. Transfer to a large warmed serving bowl and add drained pasta, reserved cooking liquid, remaining 3 tablespoons olive oil, anchovy, lemon zest, parsley, and arugula. Toss gently to coat. Season with salt, pepper, and lemon juice; top with parmesan. Serve at once.

❖ Vegetable Chili ❖

This colorful chili is amazingly hearty for a meatless dish, thanks to the subtle effect of the chocolate. If you must have meat, you can brown twelve ounces of ground beef or chicken along with the onions and bell pepper. A dollop of sour cream and sprig of fresh cilantro on each serving finish the dish.

2 large onions, chopped
1 green bell pepper, chopped
3 garlic cloves, minced
½ teaspoon minced fresh jalapeño
2 tablespoons olive oil
½ tablespoon chili powder
1 teaspoon ground cumin
1 teaspoon dried marjoram

2 teaspoons kosher salt
1 can (28-ounce) diced tomatoes
1 cup vegetable broth
3 small zucchini, diced
2 cans (15-ounce) black beans
1 can (7-ounce) mild green chiles
½ ounce semisweet chocolate, chopped
2 tablespoons chopped fresh cilantro

In a large pot, sauté onions, bell pepper, garlic, and jalapeño in olive oil over medium heat until softened, about 5 minutes. Add chili powder, cumin, marjoram, and salt, and cook for a few minutes. Add tomatoes with their juice, broth, and zucchini, and simmer, uncovered, stirring occasionally, for 15 minutes. Stir in rinsed and drained black beans, chiles, and chocolate, and simmer for 10 more minutes. Stir in cilantro and serve.

Sides

❖ Roasted Asparagus ❖

Asparagus and anise were made to go together. When asparagus is at its peak in early spring, you can't beat this quick and tasty way to showcase both.

1 bunch (1-pound) asparagus	4 teaspoons olive oil
1 small shallot, minced	1 tablespoon sesame seeds
1 teaspoon anise seeds, ground	Kosher salt and pepper to taste

1½ teaspoons fresh lemon juice, preferably Meyer

Preheat oven to 425°F. Snap woody ends off asparagus, and peel them if you like. (I feel more virtuous when I leave on the skins, with all their good nutrients.) In a large bowl, toss asparagus with shallots, anise seed, and olive oil. Transfer to a small roasting pan. Roast for 10 minutes, shaking pan occasionally to rotate asparagus. Remove pan from oven, sprinkle with sesame seeds, and return to oven for another 5 minutes or until just tender. Toss with salt, pepper, and lemon juice, and serve.

To intensify flavor and preserve potency, consider purchasing whole spices and grinding them yourself just before using. Pick up an inexpensive electric coffee bean grinder at your local supermarket and dedicate it to spice grinding. Toast your spices briefly by heating them in a small dry skillet for two to three minutes, or until aromatic; let cool, then pulverize in the grinder. (If you lack a spice grinder, crush the seeds under a heavy pot until ground.) This method is great for creating your own custom spice blend too.

❖ Black Bean, Corn, & Tomato Salad ❖

This salad is a wonderful accompaniment to grilled beef, pork, or chicken. It can be served chilled or at room temperature. It is also excellent the following day.

⅓ cup lemon juice
1½ teaspoons kosher salt
⅓ cup olive oil
1 can (14-ounce) black beans
¼ cup chopped fresh cilantro

⅓ cup sliced scallions
1 cup cooked fresh or frozen
corn kernels
1 cup diced, seeded tomato

In a large bowl, whisk together lemon juice and salt; add olive oil in a stream, whisking until well combined. Drain beans in a colander and rinse well with cold running water. Add to bowl along with scalllions, corn, tomato, and cilantro. Mix gently together until combined.

❖ Roasted Green Beans ❖

The shallots, red pepper, and mint in this dish really perk up a tired staple. Serve the beans with any grilled or broiled meat, chicken, or fish.

1 pound green beans, trimmed
2 large shallots, thinly sliced and
separated into rings
¼ cup chopped fresh mint

Pinch of red pepper flakes
4 teaspoons olive oil
½ teaspoon kosher salt

Preheat oven to 400°F. In a large bowl, toss together green beans, shallots, red pepper flakes, and olive oil. Transfer to a shallow roasting pan and roast for 15 minutes, shaking occasionally, until beans are tender and shallots are browned. Remove from oven, add salt and mint, and toss with tongs to combine.

❖ Rosemary Loaf ❖

This is an easy way to make a store-bought loaf of ciabatta or French bread a little more special. Its tantalizing aromas will make your mouth water.

1 loaf (16 ounces) unsliced bread
¼ cup extra-virgin olive oil

About 1 teaspoon garlic salt
1 tablespoon chopped fresh rosemary

Preheat oven to 350°F. Cut bread into slices about 1-inch thick without cutting completely through, so loaf remains intact. In a small bowl, combine olive oil, garlic salt, and rosemary. Liberally brush top of bread with olive oil mixture, letting it run between slices. Place in a shallow baking pan or wrap in foil, and bake for 5 to 10 minutes until warmed through.

❖ Broccoli with Basil Sauce ❖

The sauce in this dish also goes well with other steamed vegetables, such as green beans and zucchini.

Juice of ½ lemon, preferably Meyer
1 garlic clove, minced

Kosher salt & pepper to taste
½ cup extra virgin olive oil

2 tablespoons minced fresh basil

Combine lemon juice, garlic, salt, and pepper. Add olive oil in a stream and whisk until blended. Stir in basil. Meanwhile, trim broccoli and cut into florets. Steam for 8 minutes or until crisp-tender. Toss with basil sauce, and serve.

❖ Caramelized Brussels Sprouts ❖

Okay, so you're not a Brussels sprouts fan. Neither was I, until I tried this recipe. See if it doesn't make a believer out of you too.

1 pound Brussels sprouts	2 garlic cloves, lightly smashed
3 tablespoons olive oil	and peeled
1 tablespoon unsalted butter	1 teaspoon kosher salt
1 teaspoon dried savory	½ teaspoon ground black pepper

¼ cup grated parmesan cheese

Trim ends off of Brussels sprouts and halve lengthwise. In a large skillet, heat olive oil and butter over medium heat and stir in savory and garlic. Reduce heat to low and arrange sprouts halves, cut side down, in pan. Cover and gently sauté for 30 minutes, or until sprouts are carmelized on bottoms. Discard garlic, season with salt and pepper, sprinkle with parmesan, and serve. Yum!

❖ Glazed Carrots ❖

These carrots offer lovely flavors to serve with ham, roasted chicken, or pork.

1 package (16 ounces) baby carrots	1 tablespoon fresh lemon juice
1 tablespoon unsalted butter	Pinch each of mace and allspice
¼ cup fresh orange juice	Kosher salt and pepper to taste
2 tablespoons pure maple syrup	2 teaspoons minced fresh tarragon

In a medium saucepan, combine all ingredients. Bring to a boil over moderately low heat; simmer, covered, until carrots are tender, about 20 minutes. Uncover and cook until liquid is reduced to a syrupy consistency, about 5 minutes. Sprinkle with tarragon.

❖ Savory Couscous ❖

Couscous cooks very quickly, which makes it a good choice for a last-minute addition to your meal. The spices in this recipe are subtle but flavorful.

2¾ cups water *
½ teaspoon ground cinnamon
½ teaspoon ground cardamom

¼ teaspoon ground cloves
¼ teaspoon kosher salt
1½ cups couscous *

Bring water to a boil in a saucepan. Add spices and salt, stirring to mix. Add couscous and remove from heat and cover. Allow to sit for about 5 minutes before fluffing with a fork. * Or refer to your package directions for quantities.

❖ Spring Pea Mélange ❖

A quick sauté is all these fresh spring vegetables need. If you do not have the time (or patience) to shell fresh peas, use frozen, and add them in the last minute of cooking.

2 pounds peas, shelled (2 cups)
2 stalks celery, thinly sliced
4 asparagus spears,
   cut in 1-inch pieces
1 shallot, thinly sliced

1 tablespoon unsalted butter
Finely grated zest of 1 lemon
½ teaspoon granulated sugar
Kosher salt and pepper to taste
1 tablespoon minced fresh mint

In a large skillet, combine peas, celery, asparagus, shallot, butter, lemon zest, sugar, salt, pepper, and 2 tablespoons of water. Cook over medium heat until the vegetables are just tender, about 8 minutes. Stir in mint and serve at once.

❖ Roasted Root Vegetables ❖

Perfect alongside your favorite roast on a cool, crisp day.

4 tablespoons olive oil, divided
2 medium potatoes, peeled and diced
1 large yam, peeled and diced
3 large carrots, peeled and diced
2 rutabagas, peeled and diced
1 red onion, choppped

1 tablespoon chopped thyme
1 tablespoon chopped marjoram
Kosher salt and pepper to taste
2 tablespoons balsamic vinegar
Finely grated zest of 1 lemon
1 teaspoon prepared horseradish

2 tablespoons chopped fresh parsley

Preheat oven to 425°F. In a large bowl, toss 2 tablespoons of oil with potatoes, yam, carrots, rutabagas, red onion, thyme, and marjoram, and transfer to a foil-lined baking sheet. Sprinkle generously with salt and pepper, and roast, stirring occasionally, until tender and browned, about 45 minutes. Meanwhile, whisk together vinegar, remaining 2 tablespoons oil, lemon zest, and horseradish. Drizzle over vegetables and garnish with chopped parsley.

❖ Poppy Seed Noodles ❖

Lemon-scented noodles are a delicious alternative to rice or potatoes with your favorite chicken or fish dish.

8 ounces flat egg noodles	Finely grated zest of ½ lemon
1 tablespoon butter or olive oil	1 teaspoon chopped fresh chives
1 teaspoon poppy seeds	Kosher salt and pepper to taste

Cook noodles according to package directions. Drain and return to pot. Toss with butter or olive oil, poppy seeds, lemon zest, chives, salt, and pepper. Serve at once.

❖ Garlic Sage Mashed Potatoes ❖

These mashed potatoes are a delicious accompaniment to roast pork, turkey, or chicken, and a nice update to the traditional mash.

2 tablespoons olive oil	¼ cup whole milk
1 large garlic clove, minced	¼ cup buttermilk or sour cream
1 tablespoon minced fresh sage	2 tablespoons butter
4-6 Yukon Gold potatoes	Kosher salt and pepper to taste
(about 3 pounds total)	¼ cup grated parmesan cheese

In a small pot, sauté garlic in olive oil until golden. Add sage and keep warm. Peel potatoes, cut into 1-inch chunks, and place in a large pot of salted cold water. Cook over moderately low heat until tender, 15 to 20 minutes. While potatoes are simmering, heat milk, buttermilk, and butter over low heat until butter is just melted; do not allow to boil. Drain potatoes and mash or put through a food mill. Beat in garlic-sage mixture, milk mixture, salt, pepper, and parmesan. Serve at once.

❖ Roasted Rosemary Potatoes ❖

The chicken broth in the par-boiling liquid gives these potatoes a lot of extra flavor. They are so good I sometimes want to lick the roasting pan. (But of course I don't. Really.) Plan on having no leftovers.

4-6 Yukon Gold potatoes
(about 3 pounds total)
2 cups low-sodium chicken broth
1 tablespoon kosher salt, divided
1 tablespoon fresh rosemary

2 tablespoons olive oil
1 teaspoon garlic powder
1 teaspoon dried lemon peel
½ teaspoon ground black pepper

Preheat oven to 375°F. Cut potatoes into 2-inch wedges. Place in large pot with chicken broth and 1½ teaspoons salt; add enough water to cover. Bring to a boil over medium heat and simmer 5 minutes. While potatoes are cooking, chop rosemary and reserve. In a large bowl, combine olive oil, garlic powder, lemon peel, black pepper, and remaining salt. Drain and toss hot potatoes in olive oil mixture until coated. Spread potatoes and olive oil mixture in a single layer on a baking sheet. Roast for 30 minutes, or until golden brown. Top with chopped rosemary and serve.

❖ Sweet Potato Wedges ❖

This recipe uses the same technique as the Roasted Rosemary Potatoes on the previous page, but with completely different flavors. These sweet potatoes go especially well with roast chicken or pork.

4 sweet potatoes or yams, peeled (about 3 pounds total)
2 cups low-sodium chicken broth
1 tablespoon kosher salt, divided

2 tablespoons olive oil
1 tablespoon pure maple syrup
½ teaspoon ground allspice
¼ teaspoon ground cinnamon

Preheat oven to 375°F. Follow directions on previous page for cutting and parboiling potatoes. While sweet potatoes are boiling, combine olive oil, maple syrup, allspice, cinnamon, and remaining 1½ teaspoons of salt. Drain and toss hot potatoes in olive oil mixture until coated. Spread potatoes and olive oil mixture in a single layer on a baking sheet. Roast for 30 minutes, or until golden brown. Serve at once.

❖ Rice Pilaf ❖

Delicious – and a painless way to consume a few more vegetables.

1 tablespoon butter
3 tablespoons minced shallot
1 cup long-grain brown rice
2 cups beef stock, brought to boil

1 carrot, finely chopped
1 celery stalk, finely chopped
¼ cup minced fresh parsley
¼ cup chopped toasted almonds

Preheat oven to 350°F. In a medium pan, sauté shallot in butter until softened. Add rice and cook, stirring, over moderate heat for 3 to 4 minutes. Remove from heat and carefully add stock. Transfer to ovenproof dish and bake for 40 minutes. Stir in remaining ingredients and return to oven for an additional 10 minutes.

❖ Tomatoes Provençal ❖

Even people who have never taken to cooked tomatoes like these.

2 large or 4 medium tomatoes	¼ cup olive oil
Kosher salt and pepper to taste	¼ cup fresh basil leaves
2 garlic cloves	¼ cup fresh parsley leaves
1 shallot, quartered	1 tablespoon fresh thyme leaves
	½ cup dry bread crumbs

Preheat oven to 400°F. Cut tomatoes in half, gently press out juice and seeds, and sprinkle with salt and pepper. In a food processor, add remaining ingredients and pulse, turning machine on and off, until coarsely chopped. Place tomatoes in a shallow oiled roasting pan and top with herb mixture. Bake for 10 to 15 minutes, or until browned.

❖ Zucchini Slippers ❖

These zucchini "slippers" also make a great brunch dish.

4 (6- to 8-inch) zucchinis	¼ cup minced fresh parsley
1 egg, lightly beaten	2 teaspoons chopped fresh dill
1 cup cottage cheese	1 teaspoon kosher salt
1 cup shredded cheddar cheese	½ teaspoon ground black pepper

Preheat oven to 375°F. Cut zucchini in half lengthwise and scoop out seeded insides, leaving a half inch shell. In a medium bowl, whisk egg and add cottage cheese, cheddar cheese, parsley, dill, salt, and pepper. Fill each cored zucchini half with cheese mixture. Bake for 30 minutes or until golden brown.

Rubs, Marinades, Butters, & Sauces

RUBS

Rubs, made with dry seasonings, are designed to lock in a meat's juices by creating a crusty outside layer. Each recipe makes about a half a cup. You can make them in advance and store in airtight containers in a cool, dark place.

❖ Lemon Pepper Rub ❖

This is an excellent all-purpose rub. It enhances virtually any savory dish.

3 tablespoons dried lemon peel	2 teaspoons celery salt
1 tablespoon cracked black pepper	2 teaspoons sweet paprika
1 tablespoon garlic powder	2 teaspoons dried basil
1 tablespoon kosher salt	2 teaspoons dried thyme
1 tablespoon onion powder	1 teaspoon granulated sugar

In a small bowl whisk together all ingredients.

❖ Barbecue Rub ❖

This smoky sweet rub is wonderful on ribs, steaks, pork chops, chicken – you name it. You can also sprinkle it on steamed vegetables.

2 tablespoons packed brown sugar	2 teaspoons kosher salt
2 tablespoons smoked paprika	2 teaspoons ground black pepper
2 teaspoons chili powder	½ teaspoon ground cumin
2 teaspoons garlic powder	½ teaspoon dry mustard
2 teaspoons onion powder	½ teaspoon celery salt

1 teaspoon cayenne

In a medium bowl whisk together all ingredients.

❖ Curry Rub ❖

Use this exotic mixture as a dry rub, mix it with yogurt or sour cream and use as a marinade for poultry or lamb, or stir it into pan sauces for braised or seared meat.

3 tablespoons sweet paprika	2 teaspoons granulated sugar
1 tablespoon ground coriander	2 teaspoons ground ginger
1 tablespoon ground cumin	½ teaspoon ground cinnamon
1 tablespoon kosher salt	½ teaspoon crumbled saffron threads
2 teaspoons ground black pepper	¼ teaspoon cayenne

In a medium bowl, whisk together all ingredients.

MARINADES

One of the easiest ways to incorporate more flavor into your meals is to marinate your chicken, meat, or fish for a few minutes before grilling or broiling. The following marinades can also be used as basting sauces as well.

❖ Chimichurri Marinade ❖

Chimichurri is a bright, intensely flavored marinade for any kind of meat. Reserve a half a cup and use it as a sauce!

¼ cup red wine vinegar
2 tablespoons balsamic vinegar
2 tablespoons fresh lime juice
1 teaspoon kosher salt
3–4 garlic cloves, minced
1 shallot, finely chopped

½ teaspoon minced fresh jalapeño
½ teaspoon red pepper flakes
½ teaspoon Asian chili paste
2 cups minced fresh cilantro
1 cup minced fresh parsley
⅓ cup chopped fresh oregano

¾ cup extra-virgin olive oil

Combine vinegars, lime juice, salt, garlic, shallot, jalapeño, red pepper flakes, and chili paste in a medium bowl and let stand for 10 minutes. Stir in cilantro, parsley, and oregano. Whisk in oil.

❖ Lemon Herb Marinade ❖

This versatile marinade works well on meats, poultry, fish, seafood, and vegetables. Use all of the herbs, or just one or two.

Finely grated zest of 2 lemons
¼ cup fresh lemon juice
2 garlic cloves, minced
1 teaspoon Worcestershire sauce
1 teaspoon Dijon mustard
½ cup extra-virgin olive oil

½ teaspoon red pepper flakes
¾ teaspoon kosher salt
¼ cup chopped fresh parsley
1 tablespoon each chopped fresh
basil, cilantro, dill, and marjoram

In a small bowl, combine lemon zest, lemon juice, garlic, Worcestershire sauce, mustard, red pepper, salt, parsley, and herbs. Whisk in olive oil until well combined.

❖ G'ma Dorothy's London Broil Marinade ❖

The following marinade makes excellent use of rosemary and is a wonderful way to tenderize a beef top round London Broil before grilling. That means summer to me!

1 onion, finely chopped
1 garlic clove, minced
1 cup ketchup
½ cup red wine
¼ cup soy sauce

¼ cup red wine vinegar
1 tablespoon prepared horseradish
1 tablespoon Worcestershire sauce
2 tablespoons fresh rosemary
1 teaspoon kosher salt

Mix all ingredients together and pour over London Broil. Let marinate for at least 30 minutes or up to 4 hours, refrigerated. Remove from refrigerator at least 30 minutes before grilling. Grill over hot coals to desired degree of doneness, basting frequently with marinade. Let sit 20 minutes before slicing and serving.

COMPOUND BUTTERS

Compound butters are a great finishing touch for grilled or broiled meats and steamed vegetables.

❖ Basic Butter ❖

Combine ½ cup (1 stick) unsalted butter at room temperature, ½ teaspoon kosher salt, and a pinch of red pepper flakes with your choice of ingredients below. Transfer the butter mixture to a sheet of wax paper or plastic wrap. Use sheet to roll butter into a 4-inch log. Chill until firm, at least an hour. Butters can be made ahead, wrapped well, and frozen for up to a month. Slice as needed.

To the Basic Butter recipe above, add one of the following sets of ingredients:

❖ Classic Herb Butter ❖

2 tablespoons minced shallot
Finely grated zest of 1 lemon
1 tablespoon fresh lemon juice

1 tablespoon minced parsley
1 tablespoon minced chives
1 garlic clove, minced

❖ Mustard Caper Butter ❖

2 tablespoons minced shallot
3 tablespoons Dijon mustard

1 tablespoon capers, minced
1 garlic clove, minced

❖ Spiced Butter ❖

¼ cup minced fresh cilantro
Finely grated zest of ½ lemon
1 teaspoon fresh lemon juice

¼ teaspoon ground coriander
¼ teaspoon ground cumin
¼ teaspoon ground caraway seed

SAUCES & DRESSINGS

❖ Caraway Mayonnaise ❖

Acquavit is a caraway-flavored liqueur that is popular in Scandinavia. If you have trouble finding it, substitute cognac or omit it entirely. This mayonnaise is particularly tasty with seafood and smoked salmon. It yields about a cup.

½ cup mayonnaise

½ cup sour cream

1 tablespoon chopped fresh dill

1 teaspoon caraway seeds, ground

Finely grated zest of ½ lemon

Kosher salt and pepper to taste

1 teaspoon Acquavit (optional)

In a small bowl, combine all ingredients and mix well. Refrigerate until ready to use.

❖ Saffron Mayonnaise ❖

Try this take on a popular Spanish sauce with grilled or broiled meat, seafood, or steamed vegetables. One recipe makes about a cup of mayonnaise.

Pinch of saffron threads

½ teaspoon hot water

½ cup mayonnaise

1 garlic clove, minced

1 teaspoon Dijon mustard

1 tablespoon olive oil

1 teaspoon fresh lemon juice

½ teaspoon tomato paste

¼ teaspoon kosher salt

⅛ teaspoon ground black pepper

In a small cup, soak saffron threads in hot water for 5 minutes. Combine saffron mixture with remaining ingredients and mix well. Refrigerate until ready to use.

❖ Tarragon Mayonnaise ❖

This herbed mayonnaise is particularly good on grilled or broiled fish and seafood.
Or try it as a dip for fresh vegetables. It makes about a cup and a half.

½ cup mayonnaise
½ cup sour cream
2 scallions, minced
2 teaspoons capers, drained
2 teaspoons fresh lemon juice

1 teaspoon dried tarragon
1 tablespoon Dijon mustard
2 teaspoons prepared horseradish
½ teaspoon kosher salt
¼ teaspoon ground black pepper

In a small bowl, combine all ingredients and mix well. Refrigerate until ready to use.

❖ Dill Horseradish Dressing ❖

Try this tangy dressing on cole slaw. It is tasty with raw or steamed vegetables too.
One recipe yields a little over a cup and a half.

1 cup mayonnaise
3 tablespoons cider vinegar
1 tablespoon chopped fresh dill
1½ tablespoons freshly grated or prepared horseradish

½ teaspoon granulated sugar
½ teaspoon kosher salt
¼ teaspoon pepper

In a small bowl, stir together all ingredients. Refrigerate until ready to use.

❖ Poppy Seed Dressing ❖

Fruit salads and avocado salads benefit from a drizzle of this tangy dressing. It makes about a cup and a half.

2 tablespoons fresh lime juice
1 tablespoon orange juice
2 tablespoons honey
1 tablespoon minced shallot

½ teaspoon honey Dijon mustard
Kosher salt and pepper to taste
½ cup canola oil
2 teaspoons poppy seeds

In a blender or food processor, combine lime juice, orange juice, honey, shallot, and mustard. With motor running, gradually add canola oil. Stir in poppy seeds, salt, and pepper.

❖ Winter Tomato Sauce ❖

This tomato sauce has so much more flavor than canned tomato sauce. It makes about 3 cups; double the recipe and freeze half to save time on the next effort.

1 onion, chopped
½ green pepper, chopped
2 garlic cloves, minced
2 tablespoons olive oil
1 can (28-ounce) whole tomatoes

1 bay leaf
1 teaspoon dried basil
½ teaspoon sugar
½ teaspoon kosher salt
¼ teaspoon ground black pepper

In a large saucepan, cook onion, pepper, and garlic in oil over moderate heat until tender. Stir in tomatoes with their juice, bay leaf, basil, sugar, salt, and pepper. Cover and cook over low heat about 30 minutes, stirring occasionally. Press through a food mill or whirl in a blender until smooth.

Brunch – Or Any Time

❖ Zippy Omelet ❖

This omelet is easy to fix for a solo breakfast or dinner or as a way to entertain your guests by having them fix their own omelets.

Per person:
Quart-size heavy-duty zipper-seal plastic bag
2 eggs

1 to 2 tablespoons of one or more of the following:
grated or crumbled cheese (cheddar, feta, parmesan, romano),
cubed ham, shredded prosciutto, shredded cooked chicken,
crumbled bacon, diced bell pepper, sliced scallions,
drained and chopped capers, minced jalapeño, minced shallots

1 tablespoon fresh or 1 teaspoon dried
of one or more of the following herbs:
basil, chervil, dill, parsley, tarragon, thyme

Bring a pot of water to a rolling boil. Crack eggs into plastic bag and squish and shake to blend. (If two or more people are making omelets, write each person's name on a bag with a permanent marker.)

Add selected ingredients to bag and shake. Seal, making sure to get all air out of bag before zipping it up. Place bag(s) in boiling water for EXACTLY 13 minutes. Omelet will roll out easily when bag is opened.

Salt, Pepper, & Beyond

❖ Orange French Toast ❖

This French toast is wonderful served with warm maple syrup, sautéed apple slices, and chicken apple sausages. If you are serving children or prefer not to imbibe in the morning, simply omit the liquor.

4 eggs
¾ cup whole milk
Finely grated zest of 1 orange
½ cup orange juice
2 tablespoons orange liqueur

2 tablespoons brandy
1 tablespoon granulated sugar
1 teaspoon vanilla extract
½ teaspoon ground nutmeg
¼ teaspoon kosher salt

8 slices firm-textured white bread

In a deep flat-bottomed dish, whisk eggs together and add milk, orange zest, orange juice, liqueurs, sugar, vanilla, nutmeg, and salt. Arrange bread slices in batter in single layer. Let sit, turning occasionally, until batter is completely absorbed by bread, 20 to 30 minutes. (Of course, if you just can't wait, you can go with it a little drier.) In a skillet or griddle coated with non-stick cooking spray or melted butter, cook French toast over medium heat until nicely browned, 8 to 10 minutes per side. Serve at once.

❖ Baked Eggs ❖

Pop these eggs into the oven before your morning run (ha!) or let them bake while you shower. You can be creative with your herb and cheese choices for variety.

4 slices cooked bacon or ¼ cup minced cooked ham
½ cup shredded cheddar, swiss, jack, or grated parmesan cheese

8 eggs
Kosher salt and pepper to taste
¼ cup chopped fresh chervil, dill, chives, parsley, or combination

Preheat oven to 350°F. Coat 4 one-cup ramekins with non-stick cooking spray. Crumble bacon or ham in the bottom of each ramekin and top with a tablespoon of cheese. Break 2 eggs into each dish; sprinkle with salt, pepper, and herbs. Top with remaining cheese. Bake for 30 to 40 minutes, or until eggs are set and cheese is lightly browned. Let cool for a few minutes before serving.

❖ The Best Cinnamon Toast Ever ❖

Although this cinnamon toast will send your sugar levels soaring, there is nothing more comforting on a cold, rainy day. Or on a lazy Saturday morning. Or …

4 slices firm-textured white bread
3 tablespoons butter or margarine
½ cup chopped pecans or walnuts

¾ cup confectioners (powdered) sugar
1½ teaspoons ground cinnamon

In sheet pan, brown one side of bread slices under a broiler. Remove from oven and flip bread over. Meanwhile, in a small saucepan, melt butter or margarine and add powdered sugar, cinnamon, and nuts. Spread mixture evenly over untoasted sides of bread. Broil until bubbly. Let cool a little before serving.

Desserts

❖ Poached Oranges ❖

This healthy dessert can be eaten right away, but it develops even more flavor if made ahead and refrigerated for a few hours. If you want to be a little decadent, serve atop vanilla ice cream or frozen yogurt.

6 large navel oranges
⅓ cup packed brown sugar
⅓ cup water

Finely grated zest of ½ orange
1 teaspoon fresh rosemary leaves
4 whole cloves

Remove peel and white pith from oranges and cut oranges into segments. In a medium saucepan, combine sugar and water; bring to a boil over medium high heat, and stir until sugar dissolves. Reduce heat to low and simmer 10 minutes. Add orange zest, rosemary, and cloves; simmer 5 minutes more. Pour syrup over orange segments and toss to combine.

❖ Cinnamon Peaches in Amaretto ❖

This is one of my absolute favorite fruit desserts, and it is equally good warm or chilled.

1 cup Amaretto liqueur
2 cinnamon sticks, halved

8 whole cloves
4 ripe peaches

In a small saucepan, warm Amaretto and in it steep cinnamon sticks and cloves for at least 20 minutes. Let cool. Remove cinnamon sticks and reserve. Submerge peaches in boiling water for 30 seconds and immediately plunge into ice water. Peel, pit, and slice into 4 dessert bowls or glasses. Pour spiced Amaretto over peaches and garnish with reserved cinnamon sticks.

❖ Grilled Pineapple ❖

Who knew grilled pineapple could be so delectable? Healthy too!

½ cup packed brown sugar
¼ cup dark rum
Finely grated zest of 1 lime

2 tablespoons fresh lime juice
1 teaspoon vanilla extract
2 teaspoons curry powder

1 pineapple, peeled and sliced into ¾-inch-thick rounds

In a shallow baking dish, combine brown sugar, rum, lime zest, lime juice, vanilla, and curry powder. Add pineapple slices and turn to coat each slice. Marinate for 30 minutes. Grill over medium high heat until golden brown, 4 to 5 minutes, turning once or twice and brushing occasionally with marinade. Transfer to dessert dishes and drizzle with remaining marinade.

❖ Dusted Strawberries ❖

Nothing is as refreshing as strawberries picked at their peak. The cardamom in this recipe brings out an exotic note in them as well.

¼ cup granulated sugar
½ teaspoon ground cardamom
1 quart basket strawberries, hulled

2 tablespoons orange juice
or orange liqueur
Fresh mint sprigs

Whisk sugar and cardamom in a small bowl. In a large bowl, toss strawberries in orange liqueur or juice. With a slotted spoon, transfer strawberries in batches to cardamom-sugar bowl and roll them in sugar until well coated. Divide strawberries among 4 wine glasses and drizzle with any remaining orange liqueur. Serve at once, garnished with mint sprigs, or chill for up to two hours.

❖ Lemon Semifreddo ❖

Be forewarned, this is a rich dessert, and not at all healthy, I am sorry to say. But it is VERY good. Serve it in small individual dessert glasses or ramekins.

¾ cup granulated sugar
¼ cup water
3 egg yolks

2 tablespoons limoncello liqueur
1 teaspoon poppy seeds
½ cup whipping cream

In a medium saucepan, bring sugar and water to a boil over moderately high heat and cook 5 minutes. In another saucepan, gradually beat syrup into egg yolks. Cook slowly over low heat, stirring constantly, until custard is thick and smooth, about 10 minutes. Stir over cracked ice until cool; stir in limoncello and poppy seeds. Whip cream until it holds soft peaks; fold into custard. Freeze until firm, at least 2 hours.

❖ Chocolate Mousse with Sea Salt ❖

And here you have it, my favorite chocolate mousse. The sea salt brings another part of your tongue into the action, but feel free to omit it if you want pure sweet.

1 cup semi-sweet chocolate chips
2 tablespoons strong coffee
1 teaspoon vanilla extract
1 egg, separated

1 to 2 tablespoons light rum
1 tablespoon granulated sugar
1 cup heavy (whipping) cream
1 teaspoon coarse sea salt

In a double boiler, melt chocolate with coffee and vanilla. Remove from heat and whisk in egg yolk, rum, and a pinch of salt. Whip egg white until it holds stiff peaks; beat in sugar. Fold into chocolate mixture. Whip cream until it holds soft peaks; fold into chocolate mixture. Transfer to a one-quart souffle dish or individual ramekins and sprinkle with sea salt. Refrigerate until chilled, approximately 2 hours.

Helpful Tidbits

Affinity Chart

This summary of classic partnerships is by no means an exhaustive list of successful food, herb, and spice pairings. However, it is a useful place to start if you are new to seasonings beyond salt and pepper.

Beef	Bay, Chocolate, Cumin, Garlic, Pepper, Marjoram, Rosemary, Savory
Breads	Anise, Basil, Caraway, Poppy Seeds, Rosemary, Thyme
Fish/Seafood	Chervil, Dill, Fennel, Garlic, Parsley, Tarragon, Thyme
Fruit	Anise, Cardamom, Cinnamon, Cloves, Ginger, Mint, Rosemary
Lamb	Garlic, Marjoram, Mint, Oregano, Rosemary, Thyme
Pork	Cloves, Coriander, Cumin, Garllic, Ginger, Sage, Savory, Thyme
Poultry	Garlic, Oregano, Rosemary, Savory, Sage, Tarragon
Salads	Basil, Chervil, Chives, Cilantro, Dill, Parsley, Tarragon
Soups	Bay, Chervil, Tarragon, Marjoram, Parsley, Savory, Rosemary
Vegetables	Anise, Basil, Chervil, Chives, Dill, Mint, Parsley, Tarragon, Thyme

Growing Your Own

The Brooklyn Botanic Garden's herb handbook names seventy-three different types of herbs. Garden centers, books, and the internet contain a wealth of information and ideas about growing your own herbs for culinary use.

Most commonly used herbs will grow where the soil is reasonably fertile and there is good drainage. The following list contains some of the most popular herbs to grow, either outside in their own bed, as part of your regular garden, or in pots.

Parsley	Thyme
Rosemary	Savory
Dill	Marjoram
Tarragon	Mint
Sage	Basil
Chives	Oregano

Many people enjoy having an indoor herb garden. Watering plants as needed, periodic light feedings, and occasional prunings provide the needed care. Depending on whether the herb is an annual, biennial, or perennial, you will also need to renew, repot, or move outdoors on a seasonal basis.

Resources

If you are interested in learning more about the history of spices, *Dangerous Tastes: The Story of Spices* by Andrew Dalby is a good choice. This book won the 2001 Food Book of the Year prize. *Dangerous Tastes* traces the way trade routes and quests for power by various nations helped develop the culinary world as we know it today.

The following books are filled with detailed information about herbs and spices as well as recipes.

- Alice Arndt, a food historian and cooking teacher, wrote *Seasoning Savvy: How to Cook with Herbs, Spices, and other Flavorings*. Bursting with factual information about more than eighty herbs and spices, the book also contains varied and easy suggestions for their usage.

- Jennie Harding, an aroma therapist, extols the virtues of herbs and spices in her book, *The Herb Book: A Complete Guide for Growing and Using Herbs*. The book includes directions for growing herbs and using them in the kitchen as well as using specific herbs for medicines, cosmetics, and aromas.

- Tony Hill, a spice expert and merchant, offers a comprehensive guide to flavorings based on his travels around the world. *The Spice Lover's Guide to Herbs and Spices*, in addition to information, illustrations, and recipes, contains many spice blend recipes from various parts of the world.

- Jill Norman's book, *Herbs and Spices: The Cook's Reference*, has notes on tasting, buying, and storing, and culinary uses of over 120 herbs and spices. Written by an expert in international cuisines, the book and extensive photographs enhance the reader's knowledge and desire to move far beyond mere salt and pepper.

The internet also has a vast array of information and ideas about herbs and spices. One excellent resource with a super search engine is <u>Projectfoodie.com</u>. Simply enter the name of an herb or spice in the search field to access recipes from many cookbooks and most major food magazines.

Another great internet resource is <u>Food.com</u>. The "kitchen dictionary" on this site contains an alphabetical list of common recipe ingredients including herbs and spices. By clicking on the name of the herb or spice, you can find information about it and dozens of recipes which use that herb or spice as an ingredient. A wonderful feature of each recipe is the ability to adjust the recipe according to the number of servings you need.

The Cooking Channel and the Food Network both have hundreds of ideas and recipes, although not sorted by the herb or spice used. These sites also contain instructional videos.

There are many resources available to developing cooks seeking to improve their cooking skills. One cookbook that has stood the test of time is Irma Rombauer's *The Joy of Cooking*. From recipes, menus, and ingredient descriptions to table settings, cooking methods, and equipment, this book touches on all aspects of cooking.

Index

Index

A

Allspice 26, 119, 125, 130
Anise 28, 122
Appetizers. *See* Starters
Apples 36, 51, 55, 67
Apricots 51
Artichokes 109
Arugula 120
Asparagus 93, 122, 126

B

Barbecue 85, 95, 133
Basil 30, 109, 119, 124, 131, 132, 135, 139, 140
Bay 32, 111, 113, 117, 119, 139
Beans, Dried 33, 53, 55, 57, 91
Beans, Green 35, 37, 89, 91, 93, 123
Beef 21, 27, 29, 31, 47, 53, 59, 65, 81, 91, 99, 101, 117, 118, 119, 121, 133, 136
Beets 27, 29, 55, 59
Beverages 29, 37, 39, 53, 71, 85, 89, 90, 94, 99, 103
Breads & Rolls 29, 36, 37, 54, 56, 57, 91, 124, 141, 142
Broccoli 74, 79, 93, 124
Brunch 140–142
    Baked Eggs 142
    Orange French Toast 141
    The Best Cinnamon Toast Ever 142
    Zippy Omelet 140
Brussels Sprouts 125

Butters 87, 97
    Classic Herb Butter 136
    Mustard Caper Butter 136
    Spiced Butter 136

C

Cabbage 27, 29, 34, 36, 37, 59, 69, 74, 83, 115
Cakes 36, 39, 47, 75, 83
Capers 34, 112, 120, 136, 138, 140
Caraway 36, 136, 137
Cardamom 38, 126, 144
Carrots 27, 29, 33, 43, 48, 49, 51, 59, 61, 71, 73, 75, 77, 79, 95, 103, 125, 127, 130
Cauliflower 29, 43, 66, 69, 73, 79, 111
Cayenne 40, 133
Celery 19, 77, 126, 130
Cheese 31, 36, 37, 47, 77, 89, 99, 110, 111, 131, 140, 142
Chervil 42, 109, 140, 142
Chives 109, 128, 136, 142
Chocolate 21, 39, 41, 46, 51, 75, 102, 117, 121, 145
Cilantro 48, 115, 121, 123, 134, 135, 136
Cinnamon 50, 118, 126, 130, 133, 142, 143
Cloves 52, 126, 143
Cookies 29, 75, 83
Coriander 54, 110, 111, 133, 136
Corn 123
Couscous 39, 57, 101, 126
Cucumbers 59, 79
Cumin 56, 110, 115, 121, 133, 136

Curry 38, 55, 56, 61, 100, 110, 111, 144

D

Desserts 143–145
    Chocolate Mousse with Sea Salt 145
    Cinnamon Peaches in Amaretto 143
    Dusted Strawberries 144
    Grilled Pineapple 144
    Lemon Semifreddo 145
    Poached Oranges 143
Dill 58, 117, 131, 135, 137, 138, 140, 142
Dips & Spreads 63, 109, 110, 138
    Bell Pepper & Goat Cheese Spread 111
    Cheddar-Chutney Spread 110
    Green Goddess Dip 109
    Sun-Dried Tomato Pesto Dip 109
Dressings 41, 43, 73, 83, 101, 109, 138, 139
    Dill Horseradish Dressing 138
    Poppy Seed Dressing 139

E

Eggs 29, 35, 37, 41, 43, 45, 53, 57, 71, 79, 91,
    97, 99, 140, 141, 142
Entrees 113–121
    Amazing Pot Roast 117
    Chicken Dijon 113
    Fish Tacos 115
    Horseradish-Crusted Salmon Fillets 114
    Mediterranean Pasta 120
    Orange Pork Chops 116
    Pasta Bolognese 119
    Roasted Chicken Paprika 114
    Spinach Meatloaf 118
    Vegetarian Chili 121

F

Fennel Seeds 60, 111, 116
Fish 21, 33, 35, 41, 55, 61, 65, 71, 83, 87, 93,
    95, 97, 112, 114, 115
Fruit, General 21, 27, 29, 31, 36, 38, 39, 40,
    51, 56, 68, 74, 79, 83, 87, 89, 91, 94, 95,
    103. *See also* Specific Fruits
Fruit Salad 21, 83, 89

G

Garlic 62, 109, 111, 114, 115, 117, 119, 120,
    121, 124, 125, 128, 129, 131, 132, 133,
    134, 135, 136, 137
Garnishes 35, 43, 45, 49, 61, 65, 71, 81, 89,
    95, 97, 99
Ginger 64, 110, 116, 117, 133

H

Hors d'Oeuvre. *See* Starters
Horseradish 66, 114, 127, 135, 138

I

Ice Cream 19, 21, 65, 73, 103, 143

K

Kale 66, 69

L

Lamb 57, 61, 73, 118, 133
Lemon 132, 135, 145
Lentils 33, 55, 57, 69, 83, 91, 97

M

Mace 68, 125
Marinades 33, 73, 99, 115, 133, 134–135
  Chimichurri Marinade 134
  G'ma Dorothy's London Broil Marinade 135
  Lemon Herb Marinade 135
Marjoram 70, 121, 127, 135
Mayonnaise
  Caraway Mayonnaise 137
  Saffron Mayonnaise 137
Meatballs 27, 61
Meatloaf 51, 71, 91, 118
Melon 29, 65
Mint 72, 123, 126, 144
Mushrooms 43, 77, 79, 85, 99
Mustard 74, 110, 113, 133, 135, 136, 137, 138, 139

N

Nutmeg 68, 118, 141

O

Oranges 47, 51, 73, 79, 97, 100, 116, 141, 143, 144
Oregano 76, 115, 120, 134

P

Paprika 78, 114, 132, 133
Parsley 80, 109, 119, 120, 127, 130, 131, 134, 135, 136, 140, 142
Parsnips 75, 95
Pasta 31, 35, 37, 51, 75, 83, 93, 99, 119, 120, 128
Peaches 51, 143

Pears 95
Peas 26, 43, 55
Pepper 20, 112, 120, 121, 123, 132, 133, 134, 135
Peppers 40, 45, 111
Pies 31, 51, 55, 65, 67, 91
Pineapples 47, 144
Poppy Seeds 82, 128, 139, 145
Pork 27, 47, 53, 61, 63, 65, 67, 89, 93, 95, 99, 103, 116, 118, 133, 140, 142
Potatoes 27, 33, 37, 43, 45, 57, 59, 63, 67, 69, 73, 75, 79, 83, 85, 127, 128, 129
Poultry 33, 41, 47, 52, 53, 55, 63, 65, 71, 85, 87, 89, 91, 93, 95, 97, 99, 101, 103, 118, 121, 133, 140

R

Rice 49, 53, 57, 83, 87, 97, 101, 130
Rosemary 84, 111, 124, 129, 135, 143
Rubs 132–133
  Barbecue Rub 133
  Curry Rub 133
  Lemon Pepper Rub 132
Rutabagas 127

S

Saffron 86, 133, 137
Sage 88, 128
Salad 21, 24, 31, 35, 37, 41, 43, 45, 49, 59, 77, 79, 81, 89, 97, 99
Salmon 112, 114
Salt 18, 145
Sandwiches 31, 89

Sauces & Dressings 7, 21, 27, 31, 33, 37, 43, 47, 57, 65, 67, 76, 79, 81, 83, 89, 91, 95, 96, 97, 99, 103, 124, 133, 135, 137–139, 139
  Dill Horseradish Dressing 138
  Tarragon Mayonnaise 138
  Winter Tomato Sauce 139
Savory 90, 125
Seafood 27, 33, 40, 61, 97, 101, 109
Sesame Seeds 92, 122
Sides 122–132
  Black Bean, Corn, & Tomato Salad 122, 123
  Broccoli with Basil Sauce 113, 124
  Caramelized Brussels Sprouts 125
  Garlic Sage Mashed Potatoes 116, 128
  Glazed Carrots 125
  Poppy Seed Noodles 128
  Rice Pilaf 113, 130
  Roasted Asparagus 122
  Roasted Green Beans 123
  Roasted Root Vegetables 127
  Roasted Rosemary Potatoes 129
  Rosemary Loaf 124
  Savory Couscous 126
  Spring Pea Melange 126
  Sweet Potato Wedges 130
  Tomatoes Provençal 131
  Zucchini Slippers 131
Soups, Stocks, & Broths 24, 33, 36, 43, 48, 49, 51, 53, 55, 56, 59, 69, 71, 73, 81, 89, 91, 95, 101
Spinach 27, 51, 69, 118
Squash 27, 45, 61, 69, 85, 95, 103, 121, 124, 131
Star Anise 94, 117

Starters 109–111
  Bell Pepper & Goat Cheese Spread 111
  Cheddar-Chutney Spread 110
  Cit's Cauliflower Popcorn 111
  Green Goddess Dip 109
  Salmon Ceviche 112
  Sun-Dried Tomato Pesto Dip 109
Stews 24, 31, 33, 39, 43, 51, 69, 87, 91, 95
Strawberries 47, 144
Stuffing 45, 71, 81, 83, 91, 99
Sweet Potatoes 27, 69, 103, 127, 130

T

Tarragon 109, 113, 125, 138, 140
Thyme 98, 111, 114, 117, 127, 131, 140
Tilapia 115
Tomatoes 31, 35, 41, 43, 47, 53, 59, 76, 89, 91, 109, 121, 123, 131, 139
Turmeric 100, 110
Turnips 59

V

Vanilla 102, 141, 144, 145
Vegetables 27, 31, 39, 41, 43, 51, 55, 57, 60, 63, 75, 77, 81, 83, 87, 96, 101, 121, 124, 127, 133. See also Specific Vegetables
Vinegars 97

About the Authors

C.L. HANEY is an artist, illustrator, sales executive, and real estate consultant. She loves food and wine ... and therefore loves exercise. C.L. currently lives in southern Arizona, where she has grown to appreciate seventy-degree winters, glorious summer thunderstorms, and jalapeño chilies. Still, she longs to find a way to grow roses successfully in the desert.

BONNIE KEAST is a certified ontological and somatic coach with an Ed.D. in educational leadership and a work history in the field of education. She agrees with James Garfield who said, "The spirit should never grow old" and she knows that one of the ways to grow younger rather than older is to keep trying new things. One of these "new things" for Bonnie has been progressing beyond heating processed foods and calling it a meal. Herbs and spices have opened up a whole fresh world to explore and it is delicious.

Made in the USA
Charleston, SC
16 May 2013